ONENESS
OUR DIVINE DESTINY

AMORAH QUAN YIN

Edited by Stephen Muires
Cover art by Shelley Sage Heart
ISBN:1511637781
ISBN-13:978-1511637787

Once you have learned to love every part of yourself...once you have learned to love everything and everyone from your past...once you have found your multidimensional alignment...once you have fully found equality between male and female...once you have learned to love and not control people...once you have found invincibility of spirit...and once you have learned to live in unity in diversity...you have arrived!

Oneness happens when you have learned to experience unconditional love in both the giving and the receiving.

(Amorah)

CONTENTS

Mira El, Stephanie Rainbow Lightning Elk Wadell, Rondah Hornstra, Mika, Yasu, Yvonne Soderberg, Gary Kendall

PREFACE

My divine destiny with Amorah started in the winter of 1997, on my first visit to Mt. Shasta, CA. It was a very snowy day in February, and I had never driven in snow before. Gripping the steering wheel, I was wondering what other kinds of challenges I would have to face in order to meet one of the most prominent spiritual leaders in the world.

I went to see Amorah on behalf of a Japanese New Age magazine called ANEMONE. Due to the whiteout conditions, it took me over two hours to get to her house from the Redding Airport. I remember vividly how excited and how afraid I was to meet her, because she was known as an excellent psychic, and she would surely see everything that was going on with me!

However, when I finally arrived at Amorah's house, she welcomed me with an incredibly big and open heart! When we hugged, I felt like I was in the arms of Quan Yin, who is known for her deep compassion and unconditional love. During the interview, I was amazed at her capacity for peace and the state of love she held. At the same time she treated me as an equal, even though she was already evolved in her spiritual mastery. I was very much impressed with the level of her sharing her honest feelings, and how she faced her challenges.

Consequently, I decided to go through all of the training programs Amorah offered in Mt. Shasta. Amorah became my teacher for the first five years I knew her. As a teacher, she regarded her students as her equals, and she helped me face my challenges as a human being with similar issues.

I remember the very first time she visited Japan to teach, she became ill and had to stay in bed for several days. Amorah and I discussed whether we should cancel the class, and I asked her to greet all of the Japanese participants who were eagerly waiting to meet her. She agreed to go to the workshop venue with me, expecting just to greet the students and return back to rest. But to my surprise, she became so energized by their presence that she went ahead and carried on with her workshop! This showed me how committed she was to the teachings of the Dolphin Star Temple Mystery School.

Without Amorah's support, including her visits to Japan almost every year, I would never have been able to establish the Dolphin Star Temple Japan. In over 12 years of teaching in Japan, we have touched 20,000 people, including programs and private sessions.

Over the years Amorah and I became business partners as well as very close friends, until she left the planet on June 13th, 2013. Every summer I would take Japanese participants to study with Amorah at Mt. Shasta. Every time we taught together we were able to deepen our sharing of the mystery school teachings. These teachings have been instrumental in helping me to become one with my Higher Self while healing my past, present, future selves on multidimensional levels. Her greatest gift to me through the mystery school was to help me go far beyond what I ever imagined I could be, and thankfully this is still happening.

I am so grateful for the opportunity to keep her work alive, and continue my spiritual journey accompanied by Amorah's spirit and the teaching she so gracefully brought to this planet. I am sure you will find this book very exciting and helpful in activating the next level of your spiritual evolution.

Keiko Anaguchi, Japan.
Founder of DST Japan, and Certified Instructor
President of the Dolphin Star Temple Mystery School, Mt. Shasta.

EDITOR'S FORWARD

I received the manuscript of *Oneness* in the summer of 2014. It was at that point in the same unfinished condition that Amorah Quan Yin had left it at her death in June of 2013. It was in need of basic editing to make it ready for publication. Some sections read like verbal transcriptions from workshops and had the unavoidable vagueness of the spoken word. Diagrams were missing. The chapter sequence called for re-ordering. My job was to tune this up and create a coherent and unified written document. I hope I succeeded.

It was a relatively short book compared to Amorah's previous four. In the light of that fact, Gary Kendall and I started to think of making a kind of annotated version of the book. Not heavily annotated, but with sidebars and footnotes. The purpose of doing this was twofold:

1) It would highlight the core of the book itself, which are the chapters where Amorah herself speaks and teaches.

2) It would make the book have a broader base for the reader who is new to Amorah, and give it a more general and solid framework.

Some of the material resembles what has been published in Amorah's earlier books, like the contract clearing exercises in part I. Often we find a newer, updated version here in this new book.

Gary Kendall and I also thought to make this book shine more light on Amorah herself. For this purpose, we have included here two appendices in which those who knew Amorah and who were her students could share something about their experience of Amorah in person.

Today the Internet is being flooded with channeled messages. I personally do not find all of these solid and reliable. Regardless of whether I believe in the accuracy of the channeling phenomena itself, what I can do is evaluate the quality and usefulness of the resulting messages. Take the channeling from Metatron in the chapter called 'Your Multidimensional Alignment.' This message has a markedly high intensity of language; it is very structured, very focused. For me it is clear that some other intelligence is speaking here, sharing insight and information from somewhere else, and that this information is relevant to me in my life. In the book a number of such powerful channeled passages occur. They are identified by a square black-and-white icon to the left of the message, like this one here.

These channelings though are not for me the core of what makes the book stand out. For me the real power and clarity comes in the chapters where Amorah herself is speaking. She speaks with clarity and experience and a no-nonsense attitude. The chapter on Sovereignty is a good example. In fact, when we were considering subtitles for *Oneness*, I proposed *Oneness: Straight Talk and Divine Guidance*. I realize that this subtitle was too severe for a book by Amorah Quan Yin. Yet, *Oneness* has this forceful nature in some of the chapters, and those are the chapters I appreciate most.

Hope you will enjoy this book and be guided by it.

Stephen Muires
Stockholm, Sweden
March 2015

Oneness

Prologue: Eternally

In the beginning there was One. And the One said, "I Am." And One knew that He/She existed and could be aware. The One was God/Goddess/All That Is. One was joyful and filled with awe and wonder. It was as if One had just awakened from a long, deep sleep for the first time. Then One went asleep again, and awoke again, and slept again, and woke again . . .. After a time One decided to have part of itself stay awake while the other part slept. This came to pass. When the part that slept awakened and saw the other part, Male and Female existed for the first time.

When Male and Female saw each other the first time, the love was instant. They blended into Oneness again. This was deep surrender and bliss for both. After this experience, they individuated again and began looking at each other and then at themselves. They began to notice differences in the two. They were the Holy Mother and Holy Father of All That Is. Then they blended again into Oneness. And that cycle of blending into One and individuating into the Holy Mother and Holy Father went on for a great long time.

At one point when they individuated again, they noticed a specific part of themselves. And those specific parts became individualized as independent beings of light. In other words, even though they were aspects of the Holy Mother and Holy Father, they were also separate essences with specific qualities. This changed the rhythm of the cycle to all four beings of light: Holy Mother,

> By focusing on making certain divine sounds, the Holy Mother and Holy Father created individual beings of light.

Holy Father, and the two individuated aspects. They saw each other falling into awe, wonder, and deep love—blending into Oneness, then

3

individuating into the Holy Mother and Holy Father again, then into all four beings of light, loving each other deeply and with great enthusiasm.

All four beings of light had a joyful existence for a time until the Holy Mother and Holy Father began to realize that they could create more individual beings of light with conscious intention. So they did. After doing this a dozen times, they told the new and smaller beings of light that they would become the first Elohim[1]. They were also told how to create living beings of light. By this time the Holy Mother and Holy Father had determined that if they focused on making certain divine sounds while holding a specific energy. They could create beings with specific qualities, such as surrendered love, enthusiastic love, peaceful love, love with faith, love with humor, love with grace, and so on. And so creation truly began.

Everything and everyone in existence was created this way: you and me, the planets and stars, plants and mountains, literally everything and everyone. The moment each life began it was already eternal because it was a part of something that had pre-existed the creation of its uniqueness. It was ultimately a part of One. That Oneness with All That Is was absolutely magical and exciting. It was an openness to eventually explore all of the possibilities of creation: past, present and future.

As this awareness grew and spread throughout all of the beings of light, there came a moment in time when a decision about their reality was suddenly made with great joy and enthusiasm. This new reality was an instant awareness of a deep desire to explore all potential aspects of existence. What a simple 'aha' moment it was. Simple? Maybe it was the most complex single awareness that had ever happened, because then began the exploration and the creation of multidimensional realities. What lay in store for All That Is was unknown but exciting. However, no being considered the possibility that they could make a mistake in interpreting this reality, nor how that could affect them. Everything had been just light and love before that time. They did not realize that a simple misunderstanding of reality could create darkness and light, pain or joy, and eventually karma, positive or negative.

But was anything ever really negative if they could learn from it?

This is the great question that we are at the point of answering in a vast way. It has been answered by individuals who have become fully

---

[1] Editor's note: the group of light beings who are responsible for creation, also called the creator Gods and Goddesses. The first line of the Bible, in a literal translation from the Hebrew, reads: "In the beginning the Elohim created heaven and earth."

enlightened and then moved back upward through the dimensions. It is time now for all of existence to have that great awakening. It is time for us to remember that all of our experiences are an exploration of possibilities. When we learn the difference between right and wrong, it will be complete and we will be wiser. There is no blame held by anyone, ever.

I remember a time when I was leading a meditation with a class of students. In this meditation I led them into a meeting with the Holy Mother and Holy Father. Then I told them to let the Holy Mother and Holy Father take their hands and tell them something meant just for them. When I did this, I too took the hands of the Holy Mother and Holy Father. They said to me, "Amorah, you are not a failure in any way. You have never even disappointed us." I immediately began to sob. I had felt like a failure up until that time. I had always felt like I was a disappointment to the guides and to the Holy Mother and Holy Father. I had felt I was never really good enough.

They simply held me and loved me more deeply than I had ever felt loved in my life. I sobbed until it was done. My life changed dramatically after that. Of course, I still had to learn to cancel negative thoughts about myself and to affirm positive ones. My learning began to accelerate. They also said something else to me that day. They said, "When you remember that you are a beautiful being of light, you will feel our love constantly. When we look at you, all we see is your beautiful essence of love and light. And we love you eternally. So learn to see your true self, and you will be with our love always."

They sang to me the song *You Are So Beautiful*.[2] They told me that many songs by songwriters are channeled from the higher dimensions, and this was one of those songs. After that experience, my higher self started singing it to me often. I began to remember who I really was, one step at a time. I am the beautiful being of light Amorah Quan Yin. Just like you are the beautiful being of light that you are. We are all that, eternally.

It is time to remember.

---

[2] Editor's note: *You Are So Beautiful* is a song written by Dennis Wilson, Bruce Fisher and Billy Preston. It was first recorded by Preston in 1974. Joe Cocker made it a hit in 1975.

Part 1
Clearing

1 Techniques for Clearing

Before we move into the main text on the subject of Oneness, I would like to give you some techniques for healing and releasing judgments, beliefs, and contracts. The energies of holding on to these illusionary issues are causing your life to remain bound in non-truth. The chief purposes for being on a spiritual path are finding your true identity, clearing illusion, seeking truth, becoming enlightened and a Christed-self master (an ascended master).

In finding your true identity and moving in these directions, you must first realize that you are your only master. Everything you think and believe constitutes a choice about your life. Most people go through life believing that their thoughts and feelings are givens. But the true spiritual person learns to observe his or her thoughts and feelings and to choose which to believe in and which not to believe in. Self-observation is key to learning, to healing, and to becoming your true self.

In this chapter I want to give you tools to assist you in this process of self-observation and the clearing of illusions that take the form of judgments, beliefs, and contracts with self and others.

A method for clearing judgments and beliefs

1. First, think about a judgment of yourself or of others, or a belief you need to clear. Get a picture or symbol to represent this issue.

2. Breathe deeply into your whole body and think about the belief or judgment you want to clear and notice what you feel in your body and your emotions as you think about it. Observe this thoroughly.

3. Continue breathing very deeply and tell yourself, "This belief (or judgment) is an illusion. It is not the truth." Then tell yourself one or

more affirmations that are the opposite of the belief or judgment. Continue doing this until the energies you felt originally are clear and you feel good.

4. Stamp the picture or symbol representing the belief or judgment 'Canceled' several times.

5. Tear up the picture or symbol you have just canceled.

6. Put the strips of the picture or symbol into a Rainbow Flame bonfire (which includes the White Flame of Divine Trust). Burn it completely.

7. Open your eyes and go on with your day.

By using the process above, you are able to clear the belief or judgment not only on the mental level, but also on the emotional and physical level, if done thoroughly. This is important since not feeling and clearing it on those levels could easily leave energies in your body or emotions that could re-create the belief inside you.

Next is a process for clearing and releasing contracts with yourself and others. Contracts are issues you have agreed to actualize in your life in a specific way. For instance, you could have a contract with yourself that you must settle for less than what you really want, because you can never have what you want. You could have a contract with yourself to always hide from others in order to be safe. You could have contracts with your parents to be quiet as a child and never to disagree with them. You may have a contract with someone that you owe him or her something from a past life or from this life. The number of possibilities and contexts for contracts are infinite. Contracts always involve an action of some sort. According to the contract you must always live your life in that particular way. So you can see why it is important to clear contracts.

Process for clearing contracts

---

1. Think about a contract you need to clear and who it is with: yourself or someone else.

2. Imagine a legal document that says 'Contract' at the top. At the bottom it has your name and the name of the person the contract is with. This could be you, someone else or even a group. The contract says what the agreement is about.

3. Imagine you have a 'Canceled' stamp. Cancel the contract several times. If you have this contract with more than one person, imagine a stack of contracts. You will have a branding iron that says 'Canceled' which you can use to burn through the whole stack of contracts.

4. Tear up the contract or contracts into small strips.

5. Put the strips into a Rainbow Flame bonfire and burn them totally.

6. Give yourself an affirmation that will give you a new sense of freedom instead of the old limitation. Say it several times.

7. Open your eyes and go on with your day.

Now that you have these two techniques and can use them, let us look at more issues that need to be changed in order to create Oneness and to find your true self.

All of us carry pain in our bodies. Pain is energy that has died and now only causes harm. It is simple to clear.

Erasure Chamber of Light

1. Call on the Pleiadian Emissaries of Light[3] to assist you.

2. Ask them to create an Erasure Chamber of Light and to clear whatever pain is in your body, energy bodies and aura that can be cleared at this time.

3. Ask them to fill the spaces from which pain was cleared with gold

---

[3] Editor's note: the Pleiadian Emissaries of Light is the name given to the entire Pleiadian group, guardians and stewards of earth and our solar system. These include the Pleiadian Archangelic Tribes of the Light. Amorah refers to these tribes as the source of much of the channeled material in her books.

light.

You don't need to know the cause of the pain; just erase it. I recommend doing this often, at least once a week. You can also use this process for erasing psychic parasites that have been lodged in you and are feeding off the pain. They attract more pain to you and serve no higher purpose.

Further, we all have programming from ourselves or from other people. Programming is a very intense source of energy that tells you what to believe or do in life. It can block growth and block you when you are trying to move forward. Use the same process as above for pain erasure and ask the guides to erase all programming that you do not need, in order to learn and grow. They will only erase programming that you have already transcended in your consciousness.

De-possession Chamber of Light

Sometimes we all attract entities to us who are harmful. They can only attach to us at the place that is energetically equivalent to what they want to inflict on us. In other words, if you have a dark entity trying to keep you in fear, you already had fear in your body before it came in. That is what it attached itself to. If an entity is trying to keep you in self-doubt and the feeling of not being good enough, you already had some of that energy in you prior to the entity attaching to you. They cannot attach unless there is a part of you that holds whatever energy they hold.

If you have a dark entity or group of dark entities attached to you in some way, you must first ask Archangel

> If a dark entity is trying to keep you in fear, you already had fear in your body before it came in.

Michael to give you any and all contracts you have with them and then clear them, as taught above. Then you can ask the Pleiadian Emissaries of Light to use a De-possession Chamber of Light to remove them from your body, aura and hologram. Sit with your legs and arms uncrossed and breathe deeply to assist them in their efforts.

You may return to any of the processes in this chapter as needed when going through the rest of this book. I highly recommend that you also read and actively do the exercises in *The Pleiadian Workbook: Awakening Your Divine Ka*. It is the first book I wrote about how to awaken the Christed body, the Ka, and how to become enlightened. Also, the higher self connection processes from that same book are invaluable.

2 Clearing Self-Judgment

Do you love your body? Do you trust yourself? Do you have self-doubt? Do you love your emotions? Do you love your mind? Do you love your spirit? Do you love where you live? Do you love the work that you do? Do you love your creativity? Do you love yourself?

Some people think that loving these things is bad and egotistical. Some people think that all of these, or some of these, are impossible. They think their body is too fat or too thin or too whatever. They do not trust themselves to know whom to trust. They doubt every positive thought. They tighten up and repress the emotions they have learned not to feel or express. They try not to think about things they "should" not think about or are in denial about. They think their spirit is less evolved and less worthy than others. They believe they are stuck living in a place they do not want to be. They believe they have to work in an uncomfortable environment just to survive. They believe their creativity is lacking, compared to others. They go through life not liking themselves very much.

Which of these things are true for you? Let us examine each one and arrive at a bigger picture.

Do you love your body?

Most people have judgments about their body. I remember a teacher I had who hated her knees because she thought they were ugly. She was the most beautiful woman I had ever met. I could not understand it. Some people focus so strongly on how their hair is too curly, too straight, too kinky, . .. Yet others envy them the hair they have. I have always been a heavy-set woman by most people's standards. I used to be so humiliated at being fat. I would dread anyone ever saying anything about it. I felt I could die if it were ever spoken

14

about. But then one day I had a great realization: I am the Goddess that I am. I am the perfect Goddess I am, in exactly the perfect body I need to be living in. I began to heal.

We all are living in the perfect body for whatever our purpose is on this earth. We are not our bodies. Yet we live in them. There are those who live constantly on a diet, denying themselves the food they want. They feel the need to try and have a good enough body, i.e. a thin body. Models are constantly being shown to us on TV, in magazines, in movies. We are inundated with the 'perfect image.' Jokes are made about people's bodies when they are too fat, too thin, too tall, too short, too ugly. Everywhere we turn we find these examples.

Why is it so seldom that we see average-looking people in these pictures? Because most people only want to see the ideals of perfection. But what if we started to see the fat woman or the too thin man as perfect? What if we started to touch the parts of our body that we now hate in a loving and nurturing way? What if we began to see ourselves as having the perfect body to live in, without judgment or struggle? What if we would clear the beliefs or judgments we carry about our bodies?

Why not?

Do you trust yourself?

People often carry judgment about things that happened in the past. They think that because these things took place they can never trust themselves to do it right in the future. They lose the ability to trust themselves. Maybe a relationship ended. Maybe someone they trusted lied to them or about them. Maybe they lost a job. Whatever happened, they experienced it as a bad thing, and they blamed themselves for it in the long run.

Yet what if this person could choose a new route? What if when the relationship ended, they could choose to examine the details of what happened? When they first met the person they became involved with did they ignore warning signs? Did they pretend everything was perfect? Were there stages of the relationship where issues began to arise that they chose not to talk about, or even denied completely? Were they so afraid of losing the person that they hid the fear and pretended perfection? What could they learn to do differently next time? How could they create more discernment and truth?

If a person could do this, they could learn and grow and trust themselves to use this new discernment. Anytime something happens that turns out "badly," it is possible to review, learn and apply these lessons and reach a higher level of discernment. Then self-trust not only arises, it gets stronger and stronger.

Do you have self-doubt?

Some people never trust their inner voice or inner guidance. They never take chances or risks because something bad could happen as a result. I say, "So what?" We learn from mistakes just as much as we do from good results. So why not take a risk?

I had an experience with Jesus many years ago. I was in my bedroom experiencing extreme self-doubt. I could not get past it in order to do any of the things that my inner guidance was telling me to do. What if I was wrong? What if I heard the wrong voice? Jesus suddenly appeared to me, touched my shoulder, and simply said, "Amorah, the voice of God never creates self-doubt." That is all he said. Yet I instantly felt a great 'Aha' inside. I knew he was telling me that the voice of doubt inside was not my God/Goddess self. It was the voice of my negative ego, the voice of illusion.

I immediately made changes to my daily life and sat down and started a plan based on the inner guidance I had previously doubted. I have done that ever since. When doubts have arisen I have always reminded myself of that day and the great 'Aha' that I felt. I have not suffered self-doubt again for many years now.

Do you love your emotions?

Emotions are your friend whether you have grown up believing this or not. Many of us grew up with parents who were afraid of emotions. We made contracts with them to never feel or express emotions. We learned through experience that they would punish us in some way if we did. So we began to see emotions as dangerous.

However, the truth is that emotions are our teachers. They show us on the inside what is going on around the outside, and how we feel about that. Do we feel something is wrong and needs to be

> In healing the past we need to find a way to open our bodies to feeling old energies.

changed? Do we not like it when we are treated a certain way by others? We need to express our emotions so we can know these things. In healing the past this is very important.

When we have a trauma in our past, we often constrict and repress our emotions because we believe we have to hide them and pretend they are not there. In healing the past, we need to find a way to open our bodies to feeling these old energies in order to learn from them. What did we feel? Was someone not treating us in a good way? Were we afraid to challenge them? Were we frightened, and why?

As we uncover these buried feelings and learn from them, we grow and become better people. As we become better people, we hopefully learn to feel and express our feelings spontaneously, not as a way to harm others, but simply as an expression of what we are feeling. For example, we might say to someone, "Right now I am feeling a lack of trust in you because of what happened yesterday." Then we remind them of what happened and add, "What is your reality about this?" This is a responsible way of expressing our feelings that will not attack others and yet remain true to ourselves. Doing this also helps us deepen our intimacy in a truly good relationship or friendship. People need to hear what we say, and they need to act on it appropriately. If they refuse, it may be a signal that that person is not an intimate connection we can count on.

We all need intimacy in our relationships and friendships. We need people we can trust to be emotionally honest with us and who we can be totally emotionally honest with. This is an important element in our ability to heal and learn and grow. Also, it helps others learn and grow. Is it not worth it?

Do you love your mind?

Have you learned to quiet your mind yet? It is not something to judge and feel embarrassed about. Yes, our thoughts can go wild. We can learn to have a say in that and change it.

Many years ago I had another deep learning experience with Jesus. He was showing me what God's chakras were like in their higher state of being. In other words what my chakras would be like when I was fully back to Oneness with my God/Goddess consciousness. When we got to the third eye area, we entered an empty, clean, well-lit room. After being there awhile I said, "Something is wrong. Nothing is happening."

Jesus said, "The mind of God is like this. It is clean, well-lit with light and empty. That way it is always available for hearing other voices of God or inner directives that arise." I realized I needed to work on becoming that way myself. But I also needed to start being neutral about the thoughts that went through my mind and stop resenting them.

My ego-self had developed quite the agenda of always trying to figure out what was needed by myself and others and what to do to get it. I had to learn to trust more that all was as it should be. I also needed to learn to stop being responsible for others and let them grow at their own rate.

Start practicing being the one who watches in silence during meditation. The thoughts may come, but if you simply remain neutral and loving they will gradually dissipate on their own. Just don't let yourself be caught up in them.

Do you love your spirit?

Do you really believe in yourself as a spirit? Do you trust in your ability to learn and grow? Many people entertain notions about never being good enough. Others can evolve and become enlightened, but they themselves cannot. Others can meditate and be quiet, they cannot. Some people believe their higher self is not doing enough to help them. Or they believe they can never be forgiven by God or their higher self.

The truth is we are all beautiful beings of light and love. We are all good enough. It is impossible for it to be otherwise. Each of us is capable of evolving and becoming enlightened. Only our beliefs to the contrary can create a disturbed reality. Our attitudes about meditation determine whether we learn to do it or not. Recognizing that you are still learning and growing can give you more patience with yourself. Your higher self is not meant to fix your life. Your higher self is there to help you learn and grow, not to do it for you. Connecting with your higher self and deepening that connection to have more intimacy and trust takes time. And God/Goddess and your higher self do not need to forgive you. They have never blamed you. It is you who believes you are not forgivable, and that blocks your deeper connection to spirit.

In my first book *The Pleiadian Workbook: Awakening you Divine Ka*, techniques are given for connecting with your higher self. That higher self connection naturally deepens the more you practice those techniques and the more you clear energy blocks and make room for it to deepen.

If you need to clear the issues above, you can use the techniques given here in chapter 1. You are a beautiful being of light. All else is illusion.

Do you love where you live?

Do you feel grateful to be living where you are? Do you love the land that you are living on? A few years ago the guides began to stress that we all need to live in a place we truly love and are grateful for. They were referring to both the building you live in and the earth you live on.

Why? Because everything and everyone deserves to be loved and appreciated, always. They said it is wrong to live in a place that you do not like. Your dislike contributes to the earth's problems and to yours.

If you want to live somewhere else, it is very important that you do so. You deserve to live in a place you love. We all do. You deserve to wake up every morning feeling grateful to be exactly where you are. Otherwise, you feel negative toward yourself for living there. This judgment spreads out to the earth herself.

Ask yourself, "Where do I want to live in order to be happy?" In a different town or a different part of the country? Give this to yourself as soon as possible. You and all will benefit.

Do you love the work that you do?

The same lessons also apply to the work that you do. There is a saying, "When you do what you love, the universe steps in to give its assistance." This is true. When you are doing something because you think you have no choice in order to survive, you actually contribute to war. Yes, war. War is an energy that has to do with people's negative beliefs about what they have to do in order to survive. If you have adopted that attitude, you are constantly engaging in an inner war. Furthermore, if you do not like the people you work with, you are engaging in a silent war with them, too.

In order to benefit your spiritual life you need to let go of illusionary beliefs about working to survive, and working where you do not want to work. Everyone, including you, deserves happiness. So find a work place you can truly love and enjoy, and the world and you will be more peaceful.

Do you love your creativity?

I like the following definition of creativity a lot: creativity is anything that comes about through the feeling of inspiration. Therefore, what inspires you? Is it singing, dancing, flower arranging, painting, cleaning house, sewing, driving, working on the computer? Creativity is anything that you feel inspired to do. Comparing yourself to others is a tool for the false ego. Comparison to others is always wrong for you.

Each of us is a unique individual that is a special part of Oneness and All That Is. Without us that part would be missing. What we do is good enough.

I loved the book *Mutant Message Down Under,* by Marlo Morgan. It tells the story of the indigenous people of Australia from an interesting perspective. The Aboriginals celebrate each person equally. The guy who plays a musical instrument is equal with the guy who is best at catching grub worms. That guy is equal to the mother who is the best at comforting her child.

We are each valuable in what we do, regardless of what others do. Even if you are not the best singer, if you can love yourself when you are singing, you are the best at that particular gift. Learn to love what you do. Let inspiration move you to doing what you like best, in a creative way.

Do you love yourself?

What a loaded question that is! I remember years ago going to personal reading after personal reading during which I was told I needed to learn to love myself more. I got so tired of hearing it that one day I erupted during a session when someone said the same thing again. I said, "Why the hell does everyone tell

> Love is the most potent healing energy in existence.

me I need to love myself more? And no one tells me how to do it!" I was very angry at the time. What I have learned since is that no one can teach me how to love myself. Only I can learn to love myself through my intention to do so. I have to work at it.

The guides have been saying for a few years now that we need to learn to love every part of ourselves. Whether that part is a judgmental and negative voice, a past life experience as a witch or murderer, the

Mutant Message

The author of *Mutant Message Down Under* is Marlo Morgan, an American born in Iowa in 1937. The book was first published in 1990. It tells the story of Marlo Morgan's experiences on a four-month walkabout through the desert of Australia, invited by a tribe called the Real People.

Amorah mentions the book in the context of creativity: "We are each valuable in what we do, regardless of what others do." The Australian Aboriginals, like other indigenous cultures, had a respect and understanding for the unique gift of each person. No matter what that gift might be. About old people they say, "Never too old for worth."

There is a further connection between Amorah Quan Yin's work and Marlo Morgan's book. In *The Pleiadian Tantric Workbook* Amorah describes a series of sacred places on earth, called temples of the sun. One of these is in Australia, in the vicinity of Uluru, formerly known as Ayer's Rock, about 100 feet under the surface. Amorah mentions that she was asked not to share details about the location. She gives a visionary description of this cavern: 1) it is very large, 2) it was used for initiations and group meditations, 3) there is a drip of water from the ceiling into the middle of the cave, 4) through a dreaming ritual observations of other areas on the planet were made, 5) the cave was sealed off when Europeans began to reach the land of down under, and 6) there is a holographic sun in the center.

Mutant Message Down Under: The tribe arrives at the entrance to an underground site that they consider extremely sacred, so sacred that a 3-day debate goes on whether or not to allow Marlo entry. She is told that this site originally was located near Uluru, but when that was turned into a tourist attraction it was moved. She has to swear, while looking each person in the eyes, never to reveal the exact location of the cave. She is allowed in, and the first thing she sees is an underground garden, with sunlight entering from the top of the cave.

She hears the continual sound of water dripping on rock. There are many rooms to the cavern, each with a different purpose. There is a shaft down which the sun shines exactly once a year. There is a passage with murals that chronicles the history of the world. Marlo is then taken to the core chamber of the cavern. The walls of this room are of polished opal, reflecting the torch light in brilliant rainbow colors. She feels like she is standing in the center of a crystal. She is told that this room was where people went to communicate directly with Oneness.

Marlo's language is very different from Amorah's and their perspectives differ. Yet the two descriptions match in striking details.
-- *Stephen Muires (editor)*

part that cries like a baby, is depressed all the time, suffers grief all the time, or any other part. We simply need to learn to love all parts. If you cannot fully love them now, ask your higher self to help you and tell the parts of yourself that you will not give up until you love them completely and unconditionally. It will happen.

Of course, the good parts need love just as much as the bad. Love is the most potent healing energy in existence. Love heals those aspects of yourself that you have not been able to love or even like. You do not need to argue with them or try to change what they are telling you. Just focus on loving them, and they will gradually change and become integrated parts of you.

I remember when a relationship I was in was falling apart. I was miserable. I was lying in bed and crying when suddenly the word "self-love" appeared in my mind. When it did, I instantly felt the self-love pouring through me. I said to myself, "This is going to help me get through this." I have finally learned self-love. What a blessing! Start now with learning to love every single aspect of yourself and the self-love will follow.

On the mission to learn to become with One with All That Is we cannot possibly get there until we learn to love every part of ourselves and every part of our lives. Start clearing all of your self-judgments now and become more and more 'One' with yourself, integrating all parts of yourself. The rest will follow.

3 Loving Your Past

As we begin the process of returning to Oneness, which is our divine destiny, there are steps to take to get there faster. We are living in a much accelerated time. Those of us who really are on a spiritual path have chosen to be the leaders of tomorrow. We demonstrate to others how to become enlightened and in mastery. In other words, we have to lead from the front.

This chapter is about a necessary step in this process. It is time to learn how to feel grateful for everything and everyone who has, in this life or in any other life, been part of our experience. If all experience is meant to be a learning process that means everything that has ever happened to us is to be learned from. Through this we evolve.

With this evolution of spirit, back to its true self, one of the first things we have to learn is that we are not this body. We are not this mind. We are not our emotions. We are not our experiences. We are the watcher who learns from it all and evolves into the higher-dimensional self. We are the One who learns to bless it all for exactly what it is: a learning experience.

> Everything that has ever happened to us is to be learned from.

That learning experience can take on many forms. For example, I had an experience as a six-week old infant in which my father began sexually abusing me. At one year of age he suffocated me to death with a pillow.

I did die, but the Pleiadian archangels brought me back. When I initially remembered these experiences it was quite painful for me, for quite a long time. But eventually I learned to go past the hurt and see what I had learned from these experiences.

First, I learned that I had chosen to come into my family, with contracts to go through many challenges in this life. Some were experiences I needed to go through karmically. Why? Because I had gone through them in other lives and continued to see them as trauma and pain. Or I had done things harmful to others. Until I could learn to go through these experiences without holding on to them with the illusion of trauma, and see them through the eyes of love and compassion, they would be repeated.

One of the major lessons in life is to learn that we are eternal and that whatever happens to us is a fleeting experience through which we learn and evolve spiritually. Because we are eternal beings of light, everything else is just temporary and is capable of being transcended. There is really no such thing as a victim, in that we can all learn to transcend that illusion, forgive and learn to have compassion for ourselves as well as for those who did "harmful" things to us.

The victimizers are not to blame for what they did. They are simply having the life experiences they need to have in order to become better. If a person has not transcended and learned yet, harming us may be the best they can do at that time. We need to recognize that when a person does the best that they can do at any given time, there is no blame. We can see that if they had already learned and had a deep connection to their own Holy Spirit they would not do harmful things. It matters not whether those harmful things are lying, adultery, physical abuse, sexual abuse, black magic or even past life murder.

We are not really our human selves. We are simply borrowing that identity for higher purposes. When our bodies are gone, we will still exist as higher-dimensional beings of light. What we will carry with us to another life, if need be, is what we have made important.

For instance, if in this life you have made a drama out of never being deeply loved by anyone, then you will need to re-create another life of not being deeply loved until you have transcended that illusion. You will need to clear the ideas of unworthiness, undeservingness, fear of intimacy and whatever else causes you to not be loved. You will need to learn that you deserve love. You will need to let go of the fear of intimacy. If you carry the illusion that you will never be fully free, then you will find yourself in situations in life after life where your freedom is challenged. You have a need to learn that you are free and that no one can ever take that away from you, except you.

If in this life you have made a big issue out of always feeling like a victim, you will continue to create life situations where you are a victim and powerless. However, if you can learn your lessons and transcend victimhood, this will cease. If you have fear of ever speaking your truth to others, you will encounter this problem again and again until you learn to totally speak your truth to everyone at all times.

As you learn and grow and transcend illusion, you evolve. Your true identity begins to return and your false ego identity begins to disappear. We are all whole. We are all capable. We are all One.

It is time now to heal any past traumas you have held on to and to learn from them. Regardless of what happened to you, by getting repressed emotion out of your body, by learning to forgive yourself and others for what they did, you will start to grow. Take time now to ask Archangel Michael to give you all of the contracts you have with yourself and others to never forgive yourself or them. After clearing those contracts, you need to work on forgiving whoever you have blamed, including yourself. After forgiving them you need to learn to have compassion for those who have hurt you in any way. Wish them grace. Let go of your attachment for them to change, by knowing that they will do so in their own time. Learn to love them for who they really are. Learn to love them for the gifts they have given you, for what you have gained by healing and transcending your experience with them, and for the learning and growth along the way.

There are many teachings about learning to value your 'petty tyrants.' Petty tyrants are people who seem to work against you in some way. Again it can involve lying, adultery, thieving, physical abuse and so on. It does not matter what they do. Your petty tyrants are always people who teach you through what they do. For instance, my father actually killing me taught me that my spirit lives on beyond the body. I can thank him for learning that and therefore have love and compassion for him. I can also thank him for helping me become a better teacher and healer. In a way, the issues I had with him forced me to go through a healing process and enabled me in the end to transcend them.

I could not love him and have compassion for him at first. I had a huge amount of emotional trauma to heal. I had repressed emotions at the time. I had lots of beliefs and contracts to clear, as a result of my experiences with him. I managed to do this. All of it. Now I can have love and compassion for him, as well as for myself. This has helped me deepen my self-love, which is another thing I feel grateful for.

Petty tyrants

Amorah writes, "There are many teachings about learning to value your petty tyrants." Below is a selection of four of these that are most in harmony with Amorah's meaning of the term.

Carlos Castaneda, in *The Fire From Within* (1984), writes that a petty tyrant is a tormentor. Someone who either holds the power of life and death over us or simply annoys us to distraction. Petty tyrants teach us detachment.

Sheri Rosenthal, author on personal growth and consciousness, writes that a petty tyrant is someone who has the ability to irritate us and annoy us. We can allow this or we can choose to overcome this reaction tendency, stop judging and start accepting the person.

Esther Hicks, the channeling medium for the Abraham intelligences, writes in *The Vortex* (2009) about petty tyrants. She calls them 'friends,' adding that she uses that word loosely. These friends are harassing us into expansion. We have relationships that are thorns in our sides, they are uncomfortable, they give us grief, and it is exactly because of this that we benefit in our spiritual growth.

Tom Kenyon, the sound therapist, author, singer, talked about petty tyrants during the 2012 seminar *The Sphere of All Possibilities*:
"You don't have to like everyone in the sangha. It's not a requirement. In true strangeness, mirroring how the universe operates, sometimes the person that sits next to you will be the person you can't stand. Maybe they're wearing a color that just gets to you. Just realize it's an opportunity."
-- *Stephen Muires (editor)*

Everything we experience that helps us learn, grow, and evolve is something to be grateful for. The people who gave us those experiences are the ones to eventually feel grateful toward. We learn and grow from having known them. These petty tyrants become our teachers and loved ones. Maybe not intimate loved ones, but loved ones in a teacher role.

Learn to celebrate all of your life experiences, whether from this life or from a previous life. If you were killed in a past life, you need to transcend the fear you felt for the person who killed you, as well as transcend the fear of repeating the same scenario. If you were a black witch or magician, you need to explore that more deeply in order to transcend the possibility of ever doing that again. Anything you did in a past life that was bad toward others is something you needed to experience in order to be given the choice about what kind of person you are. When you have reached the point in your consciousness of knowing that you would never do something like that again, then you have transcended the karma and have become a better person.

Just like you can transcend being a 'bad' person, you can transcend blaming others. Recognize that they are just like you in the process of learning, growing and transcending. Recognize that there is a good person underneath, waiting to be reborn. Celebrate the possibility that they will eventually do exactly that. They owe you nothing and you owe nothing to them.

Call in all of the contracts you have with anyone from any life, including this one, where they owe you something because of what they did. Ask Archangel Michael to give you all of those contracts and then clear them. Reversely, call in Archangel Michael to give you all of the contracts from the past or present where you owe someone else something. Clear those contracts now.

We are all equal. As spirit sees it whether that evolution and transcendence happens today or two lifetimes from now, we are all equal. For in the higher-dimensional perspective there is no such thing as time or space. When something happens to an individual, it is insignificant. We are all on our own individual path within our divine plan. Whether we finish that divine plan now, a thousand years ago, or in the future, it is all the same in the eyes of our guides and God/Goddess/All That Is. We are never better or worse than others. We are all equal, eternally.

Let us celebrate and be grateful for this deep knowing, because what is implied is that all is well. All is well. All is well

Part 2

Balance

and

Equality

4 Male and Female Balance and Equality

Our world has existed in three distinct ways. We have lived when male and female were equal in ancient times. We have also lived in a society where women dominated men a long time ago. Most recently and continuing today we live in a society where men dominate and control women. It is time to return to equality, once and for all.

In the prologue of this book, the creation story began with the birth early on of maleness and femaleness. In that early beginning the birth of gender was the instant and total emergence of love, filled with awe and wonder, between the Holy Mother and Holy Father. We have a divine plan to get back to the innocent, yet deep, unconditional love, between all people and between both genders that emulates the relationship between the Holy Mother and Holy Father.

Believe it or not, we are capable of that great love and innocence, even in our earthly relationships, whether romantic or true friendships. But we have a lot of inbred prejudices, separation and distrust to heal first. For a very long time, we have had issues about the separation of the genders. At this time on earth, those have come to a crescendo and many people are starting to break free.

The following is a channeling by Thoth to assist you with these issues:

"Divine children, divine creators, for a great long time on the earth the role of the Father has been somewhat distorted within the religious practices of humans. This has happened within your Christianity, within some Buddhist and Muslim organizations and within the Hindu religion. There are aspects of all the world religions that have at times put the Holy Father in the role of the great disciplinarian or that of the only God—the God who watches for the purpose of judging the children, the one who watches and punishes the sinful. This has augmented the gap of separation between you and the Divine Father. These ascribed roles are not true. Even in what you think of as the sacred indigenous cultures, when disasters would happen, the people interpreted it as a punishment for something they had done wrong. The great spirit or the Great Father was punishing them. This is not so.

There is a law of cause and effect on the physical plane and this law means that every action will have a reaction or a response. This creates an ongoing chain reaction of events. It is a natural law of physicality. It is a law that stretches even to the highest of dimensions, because within creation itself there is cause and effect. It is one of the natural laws that may have different implications through the dimensions, and yet it connects them. There is no God that is sitting somewhere, pulling the puppet strings and deciding fate. He honors your free-will choices for the purpose of learning and growing. There is only a great loving God that is neither male nor female, yet is both. The Holy Father aspect of that God simply loves the creation, simply sees your beauty and loves it. That aspect is inspired by you, and sends its love, which travels on an electrical life force. He is the great procreator, the great protector, and as he sees and adores, he is inspired. You are held in that energy. Always in every moment you have the opportunity to feel the security of that great love, the depth of understanding and wisdom of the Great Father.

We ask you to be mindful of the nature of the thoughts that you hold relative to maleness. Because within original sin, within the patterns of separation that have been created and are being resolved, often maleness is seen as the one who controls, who punishes. Often maleness has been seen as the one who is violent and selfish and uncaring of others. Yet you all have examples of men who are not of that nature, who are here to be the Divine Father embodied, just as you women are here to be the Divine Mother embodied. As the past surfaces for you to remake it with present understanding, apply that understanding with compassion, with the wisdom of the heart and the knowledge of the mind that maleness is beautiful. Maleness is a divine energy. Allow the beautiful men of this world to cease having to prove that they are not the victimizers, that they are not the patriarchal controllers, and just appreciate them. Support them to be the divine aspect of the Holy Father that they are. Cease to project past experiences onto them that they had absolutely nothing to do with.

We know that there also are issues that are projected onto women in this same vein. Yet it is important that when we speak of these, we understand that it is because the patriarchy has been in control of this planet for a great long time. The dark controllers who have been charging this planet with fear for all that time are of the male nature. But this has nothing to do with the nature of maleness in general. It is simply a drama that is being played out to completion. There have been ruling and abusive dark aspects of the Goddess as well. The idea is not to put blame one place or another, for to place blame is a misunderstanding of reality and is insignificant.

Did you know there were times on this earth when tribes of women kept male slaves and sexually abused them? They forced them to give them oral sex. They knew certain substances that could be put on the penis to make it erect, and the men lived in constant fear. There are males who are still playing out this dynamic. It seems that in modern times the females who have incurred sexual damage have the idea that somehow they are more the victim than men are. This holds you back as women as much as it holds the gap of separation between male and female. It is time to cease figuring out who did the first injury and who did the most injury. These comparisons are a deep part of the psyche of the human being, and for some of you this weighs heavier than for others. Some of the men have spent many lifetimes trying to prove that they are not that way. They have played out the dark roles and so have the women. Most women have had male incarnations that were both of the light and the dark. You see, it is all within you. The part of you that feels raped is also the rapist. The part of you that is innocent will always be and has always been, and that has never changed. Even in the midst of your exploration, there is an innocent place that has never been tainted.

In your healing, the need to prove anything to anyone must cease, so you may simply be That I Am, That You Are. It is time to cease the attempt to prove your innocence to anyone, to prove your value, to prove you deserve love. It is time to cease and simply embrace the innocence that has never been tainted. This, of course, is where your meditation and spiritual practice comes in, because the deeper you go in your meditations, the more you can access that place of the witness. The witness is the place that is neither benevolent nor malevolent, but simply is. The witness exists in a place of neutrality and innocence. The more you contact that part of yourself, the more you can restore the natural countenance of spirit that has nothing to prove, has no one to blame and feels the connection to Holy Father and to the Holy Mother and to God that is Oneness at all times. You are well on your way and we give these reminders simply to help direct you toward the path home as expeditiously as possible.

There is not one among you who is not innocent. There is not one among you who has ever ceased to be loved, even for a brief second, by the Holy Father and the Holy Mother and by God the divine source of All That Is. Not even a fraction of a second has ever passed that we have not been with you. When you reach the place inside that knows that this is true, that absolutely knows that this is true, you can begin to apply this knowing to every situation in your life. Then the maturity and the grace that will accompany your healing process will amaze you, because it is the part that doubts this that creates struggle. It is the part that doubts that that love has been ever constant, that creates the illusion of separation, of blame, of resentment, of resistance, of worthlessness, of shame and of fear. When that one knowing is ever constant in your heart and in your mind, the path of returning home will be much gentler, much easier and more direct. In every fraction of a second that has ever passed you have been continually, unceasingly, unconditionally loved and seen as beautiful and adored.

Be willing to embrace that reality and change your world and the rest of the world in general. For it is so. There will come a time, and for some of you it is already happening, in which you will feel love coming in at the same time as pain is released. This will give you the strength to clear any illusion you have ever created. It will give you the strength to go beyond the illusion of hopelessness. When you are releasing, when you are feeling the pain, hold the intention of drawing in the love and the joy from your own higher consciousness, from the Holy Father, from the Holy Mother, from God, from all the angels and other higher-dimensional beings of light, because the love increases during those times. It is only the part of you that does not believe this that feels pain, to the exclusion of all else. Because you can feel both pain and love at the same time. When you come to the point of feeling both at the same time, you know that you are breaking through. You know that what you are feeling is just a fleeting energy of the past that is healing itself through your body and your consciousness. When the healing is done that love will be ever present.

We have walked on this earth, we understand the challenges of being a human being, and yet we also know the victory of spirit in human form, for we have transcended the illusion and we speak from a place of experience and a place beyond experience simultaneously. The love is ever-constant.

One last analogy: if you have a friend who deeply loves you and cares about your well-being, and you deeply love and care about that friend's well-being, and it happens that you journey across the ocean to another place, the love does not cease. The love continues. It crosses the miles and you can feel it unless you are caught in the illusion of separation by distance. Have you not experienced receiving an email or letter or a phone call or simply waking in the morning and feeling someone's love around you who is not physically present? This is the nature of the eternal love of the Holy Mother and Father. You may not be sitting at the seat of their thrones right this moment (actually you are, but in your reality it is not obvious). It is as if you have gone across the ocean. This does not mean that the love does not travel. It is up to you whether you focus on the physical distance that seems to be there or whether you just feel the gratitude for the love and send it back to them. It is only the perspective you choose that makes the difference.

When you sit and you pity yourself and you say, "I want to go home, I'm not of this earth, I don't belong here. . .," realize you are telling yourself a lie. It makes no difference where your point of origin was, whether it was in the stars or from the earth. Home is wherever you consciousness is, where you soul is. Whatever the shape, color, size or gender of your body, it is the house in which you live. What makes that house a home is you being in it and making it a nurturing and a loving place to be. Home is wherever your heart is in any moment. If you feel separate and long to go home, develop a relationship with yourself that is loving and loved at all times, and you will never feel away from home. For how can the cosmic traveler that you are, ever have an ultimate home other than inside? You could think of the soul as a portable house that you take with you, a house that has become a home.

Thank you for being with me, hearing my words and receiving my love, to the extent that you can at this time. Know that it will never cease, for I as well as the Holy Mother and Holy Father are with you until the end of time, and before and after time."

Back in the late 1980's I had a very beautiful and unique experience in this regard. The first time I slept with and had sex with a new partner something very special happened while we were making love. Quan Yin and Lord Maitreya appeared. At the time I did not recognize Lord Maitreya, and yet his divine presence was just as powerful as Quan

Yin's. They held an incredible space for the lovemaking. Afterward they told me that in the year 2012 Gautama the Buddha would be leaving his role on earth as a higher-dimensional leader and turning that role over to the two of them.

Never again would the seat of the Buddha[4] be held by either of the genders. From then on, it would be held by both equally. They told me that in order for them to assume the seat of the Buddha, they needed both males and females on earth to be already holding that equality and balance and unconditional love. Then they asked me if I was willing to move toward holding that energy. I immediately agreed, and they assured me I would be impulsed in that direction by them and other light beings until I was there. They also explained that as this new position could not be anchored in the higher dimensions until a certain number of physical human beings could hold it on earth, both male and female with each other.

Two weeks later I went to a metaphysical bookstore in a nearby town. While looking around I found a picture of the same male being I had met with Quan Yin and discovered it was Lord Maitreya. I bought the picture. The next day I received a booklet in the mail from a spiritual group. I had received it before and never read it. This time when it arrived, I felt driven to open it, which I did. It fell open to a page with the headline "Quan Yin and Lord Maitreya." It went on to read about how they would take on the seat of the Buddha and how that seat would always be held my both male and female in the future. There was only one paragraph and yet here was confirmation.

This experience began to change my life at once. I began to notice the issues of separation and incorrect thinking. It expanded greatly over the years. One particular issue I discovered was the holding of contracts by everyone on earth, contracts that had begun with Lucifer and his followers many thousands of years ago. They had been watching the humans on earth to find out how to get a stronghold on the majority or on the whole of the population. The conclusion they came to was that gender separation was that stronghold for them.

They began to work on that issue and to build it even stronger into the psyches of humans. When they felt the time was right they impulsed all humans, both male and female, at the same instant with energies that created planetary contracts. These contracts said that neither gender should ever trust the opposite gender, because if they

---

[4] Editor's note: Buddha means "the awakened one."

did, the other would take over control of them and eventually of the earth. Consequently, the males made contracts with all of the males on earth, and the females made contracts with all of the females on earth.

These contracts contained many specifications. The specifications were as follows:

1. Never love the opposite sex fully. Withhold your love.
2. Never trust members of the opposite sex.
3. Never show your emotions to members of the opposite sex, because they could use it against you.
4. Always withhold some of what you know so you can have the upper hand.
5. Find ways to stay in control but in passive aggression.
6. Always share the burdens and schemes for control with members of your own gender.
7. Never forgive the opposite sex for their negative actions.

These planetary contracts were put into place literally in the twinkling of an eye. I have worked on clearing them with many people and groups over the years. In doing so I was shown the following: when we have burned them, we can send out a command that they can be burned for everyone who would be willing to have them burned as well, on their behalf. Take the time to do so now for yourself first and then command the clearing for others who are willing.

Clearing Black Witchcraft and Satanic Males

Occasionally black magic has been practiced by groups of males and females. We are going to deal with both. Black witches and black male magicians (or satanic males) have one thing in common. They both are against the opposite gender and are very competitive. Having had lifetimes of embodying one or the other is not something to be ashamed about. It is something many of us took on so that when the time came for us to be fully in the light, we would understand what our choices were. When you have transcended the possibility of practicing black magic, you have learned the difference between right and wrong and have finally chosen right.

During the black magic lifetimes we believed that the dark was more powerful than the light. Of course, this is an illusion. Light is truth and will last forever. Darkness is simply the absence of light and truth and is an ego choice. It is temporary. If you think you might still carry those old beliefs, clear them now.

In the black magic groups we have participated in, we made many contracts with the members of each group. Most of you have contracts specifying that this connection will last forever, that you will always assist other members of your black magic group, and also that they have a right to destroy you, or kill you, if you ever try to come into the light. Often you even have contracts with the past life aspect of yourself to destroy or kill the self if you ever try to come into the light.

I had an experience many years ago that taught me this lesson. I awoke suddenly in the night feeling someone's hands around my throat. I quickly sat up and saw that the being looked like me. The guides came in and told me it was me and that I had to cancel the contracts in which I had agreed that she could kill me if I ever came into the light. I cleared those contracts. She still would not leave or come into the light. Then I was told to call upon the brotherhood and sisterhood of the ray of the ascended Christ. I was told that we can call on them for assistance as needed. I was told to ask them to take the other part of me to the sleep and dream chambers in the City of Light. She would be put to sleep and would start dreaming my life as I lived it. As she saw me making new choices in the way of light and living in total integrity, she would start to dissolve back into the light, until finally she was not in existence any more. I had the responsibility of living in total truth and light so that this could happen.

Clear all contracts with the black magic group(s) you were part of, and with yourself. Then clear all contracts with members of the opposite sex with whom you have agreed to compete and prove that you are better. They also have that contract to prove they are better. You may have contracts with others you know in this life who are still practicing black magic. This could be your mother or father, siblings, friends or romantic partners, or teachers. Clear them all.

Then ask for an Erasure Chamber of Light for clearing all black magic in your body, aura and hologram, as well as in your past lives. Give this a few minutes for it to be cleared fully. You may also need a De-possession Chamber of Light for clearing any dark entities that are possessing you due to these previous contracts. Clear all contracts with these dark entities and then do the De-possession Chamber of Light. The new freedom will be wonderful for you.

Secret Sisterhood Clearing

Many women also have associations with a group of females who think of themselves as a Secret Sisterhood of Light. They are not of the light because their agenda is anti-male. These women have experienced past lives in which they and other women were severely abused by males, and sometimes their children were abused also. These women made ancient contracts with each other, which look as follows:

1. Never trust or love any man fully.
2. Only get involved with men who are the type who try to control or harm women and children. The intention is that they can change them and keep them from harming others.
3. Always know that women are superior to men in every way.
4. Subtly find ways to make a man doubt himself and not like himself any more.
5. Hold back sexually and never give their total self.
6. Always carry the pain and burdens of other women and children as a support to them.
7. Always see every man as a dark being, not as a light being.

These contracts hold women in great separation. Many men are really coming around to treating women as equals and are being non-harmful. Many men are on a sincere spiritual path. It is time to use discernment, instead of hatred.

> Many men are coming around to treating women as equals.

Satanic Patriarchal Realm

Both men and women need to clear this one. The purpose of the Satanic Patriarchal Realm is to keep men in control and superior to women. Sometimes when males and females are about one-and-a-half years old their father comes during the night to take them in their astral body to the Satanic Patriarchal Realm. Both are taken through ceremonies of different kinds.

In these cases the women are taken through ceremonies that are sexual and scary enough to intimidate them. By the time they come back to their bodies, they have made a huge number of contracts with men. Contracts to always be submissive and obedient to men. Contracts to never awaken spiritually. Contracts to never have a Goddess connection. Contracts to never open their psychic abilities.

Women: The Satanic Patriarchal males, including the father, will have kept a part of your energy in the dark subterranean realm. They knew they could impulse and intimidate you in your physical body by keeping an aspect of you. After clearing the contracts with them, ask archangels Michael and Gabriel to retrieve the part of you that has been held there. Also call on the Sisterhood of the Holy Grail and ask them to give that part of you a healing, before it is returned to you in your body. They will take it and heal it and return it to you while you sleep.

Then ask for a De-possession Chamber of Light to clear the energy of the Satanic Patriarchal Realm and the males from your holographic energy field. Archangel Michael and the Pleiadian Emissaries of Light will do this for you.

The males who are taken to this realm at one-and-a-half years old are taken through ceremonies and teachings of initiation. They are taught not to open their hearts or their sex to women. To always be in control and dominate women. When they leave the realm that night they too have made a lot of contracts with the realm and the other men, to always be a member and to obey their rules. Clear those contracts now. Next ask for a De-possession Chamber of Light to clear them from your holographic energy field. Archangel Michael and the Pleiadian Emissaries of Light will do this for you.

Gods and Goddesses

We are all Gods and Goddesses of light embodied. These Gods and Goddesses are equal to each other. Different, yet equal. It is true that males and females have differences in their functions, in existence and in life and in their natures. What I have discovered is that each has a wholeness within him or herself that cannot be destroyed or taken away. Yet there is a greater wholeness that occurs when a male and female come into total surrender and love with each other. In this greater wholeness each will begin to see how the other completes him or her.

Female completes the wholeness of the male. Male completes the wholeness of the female. We can see in each other how the unique differences that we are add to our reality, instead of taking away from it. For instance, women can give birth. Males can be physically stronger.

Regarding The Satanic Patriarchal Realm

Amorah's descriptions of the Satanic Patriarchal Realm may sound sinister, but here is some parallel information that could put this in a balanced light.

There is the phenomenon of *Satanic Ritual Abuse*, which has gotten its own acronym: SRA. Whether SRA is fact or conspiracy theory may not actually matter in this context. Fears, fantasies and stories exist and have effect among people, especially children.

Night terrors: this is a term used for children waking up in terror but unable to respond to their parents. They keep crying or screaming for 10-20 minutes as if reacting to something. Then they calm down and have no memory of the event.

Then there is the monster under the bed, or in the closet, or burglars, kidnappers, fear of the dark, etc. Psychologists go to great lengths to explain these, ascribing them to children's lack of understanding of how the world works. But in the end there is a child who experiences fear and the cause is invisible to anyone but the child.

Christian parents may have wondered what the purpose could be for having young babies baptized, before they are able to consciously choose or decline a religion. The usual explanations include: baptism is entry into the church, and an expression of the belief that all persons come before God as no more than helpless infants, unable to do anything to save themselves. In other words, a contract is entered on behalf of the baby by the adults that are responsible for it.

We can see from this that children are indeed, maybe unwittingly on the part of the parents, being subjected to spiritual contracts of various kinds.
-- *Stephen Muires (editor)*

Women feel emotions more deeply and understand them more. Men can assert themselves more easily. Both male and female can do some of the same things, yet in different ways. Our job is to learn to see each other in the new way.

This new way is a rebirth of childlike awe and wonder, just like what the Holy Mother and Holy Father felt in their first experience of each other. We can feel that too. If we are with a partner and wake up with them each day, what if we did so with a childlike awe and wonder? What if we began each day with the thought, "Wow! I wonder what I can learn today about this vast being of light that is my partner?" Instead of questioning their actions and words, what if we could see them as something to learn from? What if we could see that our partner is both our teacher and our student? What if we could see the perfection in their uniqueness, instead of distrusting and being prejudiced?

What if in doing the above, the love and intimacy would deepen? What if in that deepening, we could allow interdependence instead of co-dependence? What if we began to realize that by being with someone who is different from us, we could open ourselves to even more learning and growing in ways we could not do alone? What a gift they could become to us! What a gift they are.

The Holy Mother and Holy Father once showed me something that was very sweet and tender. They showed me that they, as *we* learn and grow through our experiences, get to learn and expand through each of us. That learning and growing eventually spreads through all of existence and to every being of light in it. In other words, all of our uniqueness, all of our trials and errors and awakenings are shared with the Oneness of All That Is. What allows that to happen is love and divine trust.

Divine trust is something that happens when you start to look at yourself and others in a certain way. That way of looking involves seeing that everything and everyone will eventually learn all they need to learn in order to fulfill their personal divine plan. Each personal divine plan is unique and the same. The details may be different for each being of light, human or higher-dimensional. Yet the ultimate goal is the same for each: again becoming One with All That Is and loving everything and everyone. Learning to see that this divine plan is at work for each person or being of light: that is divine trust.

Discernment still plays a role, however. Discernment means that you observe a person or being of light as to what they do and how they behave. Have they evolved enough to be honest, to not steal, to not withhold? In other words have they reached a point where they deserve your absolute trust, or do they still need to learn and grow from life? Either way, judgment or contractive withholding are not appropriate. Just simply observe and let the observation be

> Just observe
> and let the observation be
> accompanied by love.

accompanied by love.

Distrust tends to be a contracted energy, a holding back. This is never appropriate, because in holding back we create separation. In radiating and loving we hold the space for Oneness with All That Is, regardless of individual levels of evolution and learning.

Divine trust affords us this luxury in every moment and allows us to deepen our ability to love unconditionally. When you can live this way, you begin to see the God and Goddess in everyone. It does not require you to hang out with someone who has not evolved enough to be honest and non-harmful. It simply requires you to love and radiate divine trust.

5 Divine Couples of the Seven Rays

Once we have learned to live in male/female equality and balance there is a special group of beings called the Divine Couples of the Seven Rays. They hold a beautiful and unique energy for the earth and her people in the form of seven rays of both male and female aspects.

The seven rays are an energy that supports us in our spiritual growth and evolution. Each of us is born to one particular ray that has a special meaning for our life and our purpose. The seven rays are Violet, Blue, Green, Golden Yellow, Orange, Red and White. Even though we are each aligned specifically with one ray, we need to integrate all of the rays into ourselves on the way toward Oneness with All That Is.

The Violet Ray is number seven and is the ray of freedom and independence. It is the unbinding of our true selves from the ego illusions of the world and the personality.

The Blue Ray is number one and is the ray of power and will. It is the power and will of your Christ self realized.

The Green Ray is number five and is the ray of truth. It is about the restoration of divine truth which is infinite. Putting an end to ego illusion is the primary goal, while recognizing more deeply the difference between truth and illusion.

The Golden Yellow Ray is number two and is the ray of wisdom and balance. Learning and growing create wisdom and absolute knowingness. This can only occur when we hold stillness and balance at all times.

The Orange Ray is number six and is the ray of selfless creativity. The main theme of this ray is that which we can conceive of and give birth to in ourselves and in the world.

The Red Ray is number three and is the ray of selfless giving. It involves stewardship and giving as a way of life.

The White Ray is number four and is the ray of purity and higher law. Universal law is the ultimate goal.

These seven rays are the distinct seven aspects of Christhood or mastery. We are here on earth to attain Christ consciousness. It does not just imply the energy of Jesus Christ. It implies the planetary office of Christ, which Jesus Christ happens to hold at this time. However, there are many beings that have attained Christ consciousness: St. Germaine, Dwal Kuhl, Serapis Bay, Mary Magdalene, Mother Mary, El Morya, and many others. These are all ascended masters of light. This means they have attained Christ consciousness while living on earth. When you too have gained Christ consciousness in yourself on this earth, you will become one of them, and Oneness with All That Is will truly be yours.

In moving toward this goal of Christ consciousness you need to learn to integrate all of the energies of the seven rays, although one will probably still be your chief expression. When you are working on integrating and holding the energy of power and will of the first ray, that energy must also be accompanied by the qualities of freedom and independence, truth, wisdom and balance, selfless creativity, selfless giving, and purity and higher law as well. Without these other qualities being at least partially present, it is not possible to embody the divine power and will of the Blue Ray. In other words, the seven ray energies work best when in synergy with one another.

The Divine Couples of the Seven Rays work in this synergistic way with their partners, but also with the whole of the group. In working with them during group meditations, it has happened in the last two years that they sometimes became a collective voice for channeling. They retain their individual characteristics. However, they also hold the deep connection with all of the other couples.

I would like to now introduce them to you one couple at a time. They will each bring through a channeling about the male or female aspect of their particular ray.

Quan Yin and Lord Maitreya are the divine couple of the Violet Ray. They work together as keepers of this ray.

Quan Yin speaks, "As the female energy of the Violet Ray I am honored to speak to you. But first I wish to say that without the divine male energy, my anchoring of the seventh ray would not be complete. So I only speak about the nature of the female energy that could not exist without the male, and vice versa. We are equal but individual. We are whole and only half of the whole at the same time, paradoxically.

As the female energy of the Violet Ray I hold the quality of independence that also surrenders to interdependence. I know that I have a wholeness inside myself. I also know the greater wholeness that is male and female together. For instance, as I hold the surrender to interdependence, it allows the male to act on that interdependence in whatever way is appropriate. I also hold the quality of freedom that can only exist when

> My freedom is absolute.

my thinking and choices are valued by the male and by others. In other words, my freedom is absolute. Yet I have surrendered that individual freedom to a mutual freedom with the male. I trust myself implicitly, as I trust Lord Maitreya implicitly. Therefore neither of our freedoms is ever sacrificed or compromised. However, this freedom is a shared commodity."

Lord Maitreya speaks, "As the male keeper of the Violet Ray I hold a quality similar to Quan Yin and yet different. For instance, as she said above, as she surrenders to interdependence it allows me to act on it. This surrender allows me to state absolutes about what independence really means to an individual and how to act on that. When the female surrenders to the freedom that we share, this surrender holds the space for me to act on that freedom in the way of guidance to others. It assists me in guiding others toward valuing their own freedom and understanding what freedom truly is. Freedom is being unbound by anything other than what you independently know to be right and true."

Jesus Christ and Mary Magdalene are the divine couple of the Blue Ray.
Mary Magdalene speaks, "The process of developing your divine power and will entails a constant assessment of what that power and will really mean. I hold the energy of the surrender of having that power and will over others, and holding it only for myself. I hold patience and forgiveness for the inappropriate use of power and will by others, while holding pure discernment. In other words, I know the importance of using discernment and helping others to trust their own discernment as it is developing."

Jesus Christ speaks, "Having power involves deep self-knowing. Until you can trust yourself to always choose what is right in every situation, you cannot have true divine power. With true divine power you are the ruler and chooser of all things in your life, but never in the life of others. Honoring the free will of others is primary to having power. It also makes sure that your actions will always be based on the surrender of the female aspect to divine will. Then you can use your will to create and act in a moral and selfless manner."

Tara and Chen-Resi[5] are the divine couple of the Green Ray.

Tara speaks, "Hello beautiful ones, I am Tara and I hold the energy of the divine feminine Green Ray of truth. I can help you trust your inner knowing of what is truth and what is illusion. That knowing comes from being in your center and as much in your silence as is possible. When you think about something and you are deciding if it is truth or illusion, go inside that deep centered place to think about it. What do you feel? If you feel contraction or a pulling back, it is illusion. If you feel a deep opening or a deep breath, it is truth. Absolute truth is infinite. Your changing reality is not absolute truth, it is only temporary."

Chen-Resi shares, "The divine masculine energy of the Green Ray acts on truth. I can help you in your quest to always speak truth to others and to yourself. Many people hold back their truth in an effort to be accepted by others. They fear to speak their truth because of the response it might bring from others. However, the true spiritual person always speaks truth spontaneously and does not care about the response of others. Sharing your truth is a great gift to others, whether they realize it or not. If they do not, then the appropriate reaction for you is simply to feel compassion for them in their ongoing process of learning and growing. Always trust that they will evolve and come to know truth eventually. All will."

Next to speak is Deodata of the Golden Ray. She says, "In order to anchor the space of wisdom and balance I live in a state of great trust. I certainly trust in my divine

---

[5] Editor's note: Chen-Resi is the Tibetan name for the being called Avalokiteshvara in Sanskrit.

counterpart. I also hold the wisdom and balance to recognize that all beings are equal and of the light. I watch your life process and how you evolve in stages and I trust that you will eventually join us in our higher-dimensional mastery of the light. Even though it is not obvious at the moment, I trust that this is true. I trust and hold patience with an inner knowingness that, however long it takes, we all have eternity to experimentally move through life. It is inevitable that you again become your true self."

Gautama the Buddha, keeper of the Golden Ray, iterates, "I speak to you at this time from a place of divine masculine energy and from the gifts I hold for you in that regard. Holding divine balance is an act of truly mastering the art of being in your center and having the wisdom that comes from having transcended being in reaction to what goes on around you. Acting on inner wisdom is a spontaneous response to life and surroundings. In this inner wisdom, you have learned to live in the balance of who you truly are and to see illusion for what it is: simply an opportunity for people to experience, learn, and become better. Therefore: no reactions or judgment ever. Acting on your wisdom is only dependent on yourself being who you are and acting wisely because you know inside what is right and what is wrong."

Radha of the Orange Ray speaks, "As Goddess of the Orange Ray, I share the energy of inspiration that brings creativity. It is not contrived in any way to get a specific reaction from others. It comes from deep inside me, and you, from the core of the soul and what you feel in your soul, from inspiration. Whether it involves the birth of a child, the birth of a new way of being, an act that is artistic or an act that is giving from the heart and soul, I help you find that deeply held energy of soul inspiration that brings about whatever creativity is your natural gift from God/Goddess. Can you simply gaze upon a fresh flower or a grain of sand and see creation in its fullness? Is your soul inspired by this?"

Krishna speaks as the divine male of the Orange Ray, "Brothers and sisters, all of life is a celebration. All of life is inspiration to create as an expression of your soul sharing itself with All That Is. This form of creativity comes from a deep place inside where you know who you are and what creation is. You must realize that this brings an expression of joy from the soul. In the traditional stories about me, I play the flute and others simply follow because of the inspiration it awakens in them. My playing the flute is a constant expression of my soul and its own inner awakening. Know that letting that part of yourself share with others helps them to access their own selfless creativity."

White Buffalo Calf Woman shares about her role as the divine female of the Red Ray, "Great and humble ones, we are all on earth to experience stewardship of the earth and of everything physical in our lives. We must learn to honor the beauty in All That Is and in each other. We must remember that the earth and our physical possessions outlive us. So how can we own it? We can partake of earth's gifts such as food and shelter, clothing and warmth. Being humble requires us to live in the deep understanding that we did not create these things. The earth did. When you partake of them, always give thanks to earth and to the God/Goddess All That Is for providing you with all that you need."

Hiawatha of the Red Ray speaks, "Brothers and sisters, as stewards of the earth we must care for her in every way possible. It goes against divine law to pollute the earth, to destroy her in any way, to be greedy. To think we own the earth or anything of her is a great ego illusion. We are earth's caretakers. The earth is plentiful enough for all people's needs to be met. Yet the social ways of her people are based on greed and ownership. This must eventually change in order for you to live in harmony again with the earth and others. Refuse to use products that are polluting the Great Mother. Production of all plastics, fuel burning, using perfumes and detergents and so on, all cause harm to earth and her people[6]. No more dumping trash and waste into the waters and into the earth's body. Love and protect her in all ways. Live in a natural way with the earth and receive her love every day."

Shakti is the divine female of the White Ray. She says, "Beautiful beings of light, I say to you that you are eternally pure. Yes eternally! You have chosen to forget and re-remember through having third-dimensional life. You have chosen to live many forms of life and to learn and grow from them.

---

[6] Editor's note: Amorah herself was committed to using natural products and fragrance-free hygiene. During workshops she insisted that all participants use on scent-free soap.

However, some of you have held beliefs that you have lost your purity, and this is not true. Some of you have been violently or sexually abused, and feel this has destroyed your purity and innocence. But I tell you now this is not the truth. You have the ability to heal these issues and learn from them. Even if you have killed a person in another life or practiced black magic, this simply gave you life experiences that you can transcend the capacity of ever repeating. Why? Because at the core of your soul and beingness you are pure."

Osiris tells his story, as the divine male of the White Ray: "Greetings to you. I want to tell you a story from the traditions about me. The story goes that I was once conquered on earth and cut into many pieces. Those pieces were scattered all over the earth and wholeness was lost. When my mate discovered this, she began to locate these scattered parts and attempted to put them back together. She did this with all but the final part, which I then had to find and reattach. Only I could do it. This story is symbolic in its nature. It represents how when we come to earth we begin to develop an ego that separates us from our true selves. The cut up pieces represent this division of the true self. In order to find our true selves again, we go through many life experiences from which we gain knowledge and understanding. Eventually, just living life is not enough and we enter the spiritual quest for absolute truth. That quest leads us to reassemble our physical and higher-dimensional selves. In that final step we move into mastery as the true self that is invincible and has never lost its purity. We join into Oneness with all parts of ourselves and with All That Is."

These Divine Couples of the Seven Rays have shared with us our own divine qualities that are eternally part of us. When we regain them all, all seven rays worth, we have re-become our Christed self and regained our relationship with All That Is. Which we never really lost. We simply hid it from ourselves for a time.

6 Living as Helpmates

Living as helpmates is a divine way of life for couples, but also for intimate friends. It is a way of co-creating loving and divine trust-based relationships in life. For this to work both people involved must agree. It is a commitment toward assisting each other in learning and growing and becoming fully enlightened. In other words, both people need to be 100% committed to their own spiritual path first. They both must have learned how to monitor their thoughts and feelings and to choose truth. That commitment to trust must also be absolute. The commitment to changing as they learn and grow must be absolute.[7]

When a person has this commitment, you can observe them learning and growing and changing. You can trust them to be working on being the best that they can be. When you have that level of trust in a person, becoming helpmates is possible.

Becoming helpmates means that you can give them feedback about something they do that affects you, sometimes in a negative way. When

> Share what you feel,
>
> in a non–blaming way

you share this with them, you do so in a non-blaming way, sharing what you feel. Then you need to ask them what their reality is. This helps you in not taking things personally. You can do this because you have watched how they can ingest feedback and use self-observation to change as is needed. They have earned your trust in an absolute way.

You are also able to share with them your deepest issues. You know that there is nothing to be ashamed of, because the negative

---

[7] Editor's note: Amorah called herself and others sometimes to very high standards that are difficult to live up to.

experience happened in order to assist you in learning and growing. You developed trust that they will not judge you. They will simply love and support you and hold the space for your learning and growing. You do that for each other. In other words, there ceases to be a reason for keeping quiet about issues, and this allows you to always be spontaneously and emotionally truthful. What a blessing!

They can do the same thing with you. You listen to them with an open heart, never judging, genuinely caring about their reality and what they are feeling and learning. You really want them to grow and evolve, and how they choose to do it is your great joy. You can believe them and what they say, because you have learned that deep, absolute trust.

Being helpmates also involves seeing them constantly as a God or Goddess embodied, a being that is of the light. You want them to be the best that they can be and you see them as being that in every moment along the way. You see them as a living testimony to trust, love, and actualization of truth. You see them as loving you in the same way.

Sexuality as well needs to evolve into a tantric relationship. Tantra is a special kind of sexual intimacy in which both parties learn to allow the sexual energy to move upward through the chakras. This assists both parties in bringing about a state of ecstasy. Jesus has shared with me that to be an ascended being of light means living constantly in a state of ecstasy. There will be no resistance, only surrender and allowing. That comes from deep and intimate love. There is nothing to hide from yourself or your partner.

In tantric sexuality you learn to take your lovemaking to a whole new level. There is no longer any lust-based sexual energy. You learn to see each other's God or Goddess self. You learn to give to and receive from that beautiful soul. You look at them and feel a deep desire to give to them because they deserve it completely. They do the same for you. You do not go into this for the purpose of receiving and getting. You enter into the lovemaking from a space of genuinely wanting to express your love, devotion, and adoration for the other person. You want to give. You want to surrender deeply to their giving to you. After all they are a God or Goddess embodied. How could you not surrender to that?

The combination of love and surrender create the tantric bliss. You can at the end of the experience see and feel yourself as the entire universe embodied. Sometimes you may feel yourself as Oneness embodied. Sometimes you may experience yourself as a dolphin or whale spirit. These special experiences are not a vision. You actually become this expanded thing for a time. When you do expand into this higher state, you experience the role the partner is playing in this. Is he the love of God filling that universe and bringing it to life? Is she the universe coming to life as you love her? I have had these types of experiences with a partner. I know they are real.

Lust-based sexual energy comes out of an inner need to take and have power over. Lust and pornography create dark entities in your second chakra that lead you to more lust. This must stop at once. Clear the contracts and do a De-possession Chamber of Light. Begin now changing your beliefs and ways of thinking about sexuality. If need be, decide on a time of celibacy in order to achieve this new state of being ready for a loving tantric relationship.

There are some practices of tantra that only benefit the male. Buddhist tantric practice is often this way. The man uses the tantric practice to increase his own energy while the female only serves him and does not receive the tantric awakening. However, true tantra is mutual and equal between the male and female. True tantra is not just a technique. It is based on deep love, trust and surrender. Only then can it bring the great awakening that is intended.

My third book is entitled *The Pleiadian Tantric Workbook: Awakening Your Divine Ba*. Ba is an ancient Egyptian word that means 'soul.' In order to work with that book you need to have finished the workbook entitled *The Pleiadian Workbook: Awakening Your Divine Ka* first. This can be very helpful in healing the male/female issues, and in learning about tantra and becoming fully realized helpmates.

7 Procreation

This is a channeling from the collective voice of the Elohim.

אֱלֹהִים "In the name of the mighty and beloved I Am Presences of those whom you call the Elohim, we wish to speak to you as a collective voice of the One Elohim, as a council of creators and sustainers of creation, as the nurturers of creation. We are the ones that anchor those who are in the constant rhythm of individuation and merging into Oneness, with each other and with All That Is. We are those who hold the rhythm of creation that exists throughout all of creation. Yet we are not All That Is, and yet we have a relationship with All That Is that is unique, as those who have given birth to you, as those who have helped your unique essence find an individuated expression, and as those who have celebrated the variations on the theme of creation, through the very uniqueness that you express.

All of existence was simply a consciousness at one time. Within that consciousness the desire to explore the nature of All That Is, and all that is possible, was born in stages. It was like a passionate desire, like a childlike curiosity that was filled with awe and wonder. As the divine plan to fulfill that longing to understand the potentials of existence began to be realized, there were levels of hierarchical dispersing of responsibility. Yet those original responsibilities were based on the uniqueness of the quality of the essence of each and every creator being. Let me say that again. Every area of responsibility was birthed from a place of the natural expression of the unique and individual qualities of each and every being. When a being who most strongly held the quality of divine innocence was created within the Elohim, or archangelic realms, or the realm of what some call the overlords, then the natural tendency of those beings within that creation was to recognize, uphold and nurture innocence in others. It was the place where the frequency matched most exactly.

The Elohim of divine innocence were also very loving beings, and beings who had a connection to the mind and wholeness of God, and to the passion for creation, and to the joy and the peace. Yet, their most outstanding frequency was the frequency of innocence. You might think of them as the birthers or the distributors or the ones that care, the creators on that frequency level. The Elohim and archangels and overlords of divine love, or divine rapture and all of the other qualities, had specific areas that were natural for them to hold within creation, simply because of what they were.

When creation began there was not even an understanding that the creators would need to somehow take care of creation. It was simply an exploration into the levels of consciousness and individuation that existed. In the beginning it was not necessary to take care of it, until existence began to spread out, so to speak, into further and further dimensional realms. Then it became clear, for instance, that those on the fifth-dimensional realm needed connection with beings on the sixth- through twelfth-dimensional realms, in order to connect back to source, to connect to the angels, to connect to the Elohim.

Within all of creation it was a great experiment. We were learning, as we created, about the nature of the potentials of existence. We were also learning that with that creation came a certain responsibility, and that for Oneness to remain in Oneness there needed to be communication and linkage between all dimensional realities and the consciousness within them. It was a great adventure that covered, in your terms, what you might think of as millions and millions of years of simply discovering the kinds of realities in which each being would enjoy participating and would naturally be drawn to participate in. There was curiosity about the potential of how many different realms could be created, and how many different environments a single being could experience. Even within the Elohim, the archangelic and the overlord realms themselves, beings began to experiment with creating things that were within their own consciousness, instead of being separate, until many of us came into the human realm.

Yet, some of the reason for that was not always inspired by curiosity. There were times in the creation process and the experimentation in which we overstepped our bounds, as parents sometimes do. In your lives, when you have parents who overstep their authority, you are experiencing that because somewhere in your higher-dimensional realm somewhere along the way you either experienced being a creator being who overstepped the bounds and the care-taking of creation, or you experienced that happening to you through the beings who created you. This dynamic was intended to be that of the parents learning to simply hold the child in love, and allowing it to explore the nature of its own reality with free will, and yet teaching it about benevolence, how to recognize what is right or wrong, teaching it ways of being healthy, and so on. Then, as the child reached a certain age, or actually many different ages, the parents would let go of imposing those teachings and allow the child to choose whether it would live by what has been shared, or create a whole new reality of its own.

Each and every one at every level has a creative potential: through thought, through emotion, through visualization or through sexual energy.

Some of you have experienced parents who were in such overload and karmic issues in their own lives that they perhaps did not take appropriate levels of responsibility for you. Perhaps you felt neglected. There were stages in the creation process in which the Elohim, the archangels and the overlords had created something and then moved on. Those parts of creation at times did feel a level of separation, abandonment or neglect from the creators, from God, from Source, until we began to realize that things were not working, and that we needed to give it more creative energy until it was ready to stand on its own.

What we are here to explain to you today is that the very nature of parenting is one for which we were not

> In the process of returning to divine flow it is necessary to comprehend the innocence born of ignorance.

really prepared, because it was an unknown. On this earth very few people are totally prepared. Mistakes are made, if you can call it a mistake to be doing all you know to do until you learn more. The potentials of creation are vast. We have learned over time that our role within creation varies from one moment to the next. We have learned that within the reality of creating other beings of light and consciousness, to break away from our own divine flow in order to sustain or to bring healing, is a breach in the integrity of existence. Yet there are times when things need to be dealt with very quickly, and then it is very natural and loving to do so.

In the process of returning to divine flow it is necessary to comprehend the innocence born of ignorance, which has permeated existence for a vastly long time. Yet from the best that we can understand at this time, it appears that most, or all, of the potentials for reality and for individuals have been explored in one way or another. Even though you may have a desire to return to divine flow, there are still those who have a desire to resist it, and we will not interfere with those beings. We, and all of the higher-dimensional beings of light on all levels, have been learning over eons, and millions and billions of years of time, that until an individuated consciousness has experienced everything it wishes to experience, and then of its own free will and accord chooses to turn toward home on a divine flow level, that it is not ours to interfere with their choices. For within each of these beings the desire to explore the potentials of reality was birthed from their own parenting. The things that we have perceived as disasters in the past, the things that we have perceived as great disruptions to creation, have all been sorted back to a level of understanding that it is just another potential of reality being experienced by beings of light who are exploring. Now it is done, and we can move to something else.

We have been humbled many times by our overreactions to the creation, and have had to take a step back many times, to re-look at our own perceptions, and return to divine flow. We have spent eons learning how to respond to people's desperation and to their prayers, without interfering with their free will.

There has never been an intentional neglect, or an intentional overstepping of authority, or an intentional lack of love, in any way. Yet those who are on the other end of this reality have chosen to perceive it in that way at times, because of the interdependence that exists within the dimensional realities. Beings who exist on a lower frequency dimensional level have created a belief in a dependency on higher-dimensional beings that is beyond what is real. At the same time there is a healthy interdependence in All That Is, because All That Is is on an ultimate level: Oneness."

An exploration into the meaning of Oneness and individuation

We invite you now to close your eyes and take a few full-bodied breaths to bring yourself into presence. We want to take you on a little journey of exploration into the meaning of Oneness and individuation. So take a moment to align with your own inner beingness, deep in your heart, deep in your body.

Begin with the affirmation, three times, "I Am the One That I Am." Say it to yourself, keep it inside, and notice what you feel as you say the affirmation, "I Am the One That I Am." Continue silently repeating these words, as you breathe into your toes and feet, and see if you can feel the words penetrate your toes and your feet, or if there are places in that part of your body that resist those words. Do this and observe.

Breathing into your toes and the feet, say the affirmation, two or three times, "I am deeply loved by All That Is," and notice if your toes and your feet accept and receive those words. If there is a place in your body where you feel a pain, or a tightness, or a numbness, just make a mental note of it.

Bring your awareness to the calves of your legs, to your shins, while affirming "I Am the One That I Am." Do this while breathing into that part of your body and noticing the response. Continue to breathe into your calves and your shins, affirming, "I am loved by All That Is."

Next breathe into your knees, "I Am the One That I Am." "I am loved by All That Is."

Breathe into your thighs, and from the top of the knees up to the hips, "I Am the One That I Am." "I am loved by All That Is." Keep making a mental note of the places in the body that have a reaction, that are not fully receiving the words and the message.

Now breathe into your hips, your buttocks, "I Am the One That I Am." "I am loved by All That Is."

Breathe specifically into your genitals, "I Am the One That I Am." "I am loved by All That Is."

Breathe into your abdomen, and your belly and your pelvis, "I Am the One That I Am," and, "I am loved by All That Is."

Breathe into your upper torso in the front, your chest, the front of your ribs, your breast and the front of your shoulders, "I Am the One That I Am." "I am loved by All That Is."

Breathe into your back from the waist up, and into your shoulder blades, "I Am the One That I Am." "I am loved by All That Is."

Breathe down your arms to your fingertips, affirming, "I Am the One That I Am," observing where your arms receive the message, and where they do not. Observe your hands and your fingers. "I am loved by All That Is."

Breathe into your throat and your head, "I Am the One That I Am."

Let your mouth be open a little. Breathe into your whole head, your ears, your eyes, your nose and your mouth. Take about four or five breaths while focusing on different areas. "I Am the One That I Am." Imagine those words penetrating your entire face, and notice what you feel there. Begin at the throat again, "I am Loved by All That Is." Expand those words into the head, into your cranium, into your brain, into your ears and your eyes.

Now begin deep full-body breaths. As you inhale bring your breath deeply into your arms and fingers, torso, legs and feet, all in one deep breath. Then exhale out through the pores of your skin, radiating your breath and essence energy out into your auric field. After doing this a couple of times, continue this form of breathing while affirming, "I am loved by All That Is. I Am the One That I Am."

[Amorah continues:] The Elohim channeling above has demonstrated how the first experiences of parenting were on a higher-dimensional level. Yet there is much to be learned from what they shared. As parents you are given a blessing and an opportunity to bring a new being of light into the world. It is your job to love them always and to resist the temptation to make them be what you think they should be. In raising a child you are expected to give guidance and direction when they are younger. You are also expected to let them experiment with their choices in life and to find out what they want.

Your children are unique individual beings of light, embodied in order to learn and grow just like you are. You must allow them to do so in their own way. You are not meant to control them. You are meant to hold the space for their learning and growing in their own way. They are not yours. You simply gave them assistance in coming here and protected them during their early years. What they do along the way and afterward is their business, not yours.

Always remember that worrying about them is like a negative criticism. It is like saying, "You poor thing. You are not capable of learning and growing in this life. I need to do it for you." Yet, of course, they are capable of doing it themselves. They are capable of learning and growing along the way. Worry is a negative ego reaction. Love, compassion and support are the way of a truly good parent.

Remember you are not their creator. You are simply the vehicle they chose to come into human life through. Honor and respect them accordingly

Part 3

Spiritual

Mastery

8 Transcending Light and Dark

Some of us who are very sensitive may have experiences of 'dark beings' invading us or trying to create negative realities for us. We need to realize that they could not even be connecting to us if we did not have a frequency inside us that corresponds to the one they are attempting to send to us. We created that situation. They are a product of our ego imagination gone awry. At this point you need to clear any and all contracts you have made with them in the

> Dark energy is dependent upon your belief that it has power.

past. Then ask for a De-possession Chamber of Light and command it in the name of Christ consciousness and your own universal free will (see the description in chapter 1 on clearing techniques).

Being afraid of these beings of darkness gives power to the illusion of ego and the experiences it has created.

Light is eternal and light is truth. Darkness is a product of illusion that we must transcend. It is not more powerful than light. Light is ultimately more powerful than dark. Reclaim your freedom from these illusions fearlessly and clear any beliefs you are holding about them. With the power of Christ consciousness and universal law as your deep trust, you are harmless and can remain unharmed.

Dark energy is dependent upon your belief that it has power. Part of becoming awakened and enlightened is to transcend this belief and to learn to only see and believe in the trust which is beyond all things dark.

Below is a channeling from Mother Mary, which can help you

understand this new way of looking at reality as well as help you in the process of becoming the best that you can be.

Mother Mary speaks: "When the one you know as my son and I experienced the initiation into death and resurrection together in Egypt, the one you call Jesus the Christ was 18 years of age. When we visited the temples in Egypt for that final initiation, the procedure was to seal the initiate in a sarcophagus in a chamber beneath the surface of the earth. During this initiation, which was spoken of in *Pleiadian Perspectives on Human Evolution*[8], we had to cross the isle of crocodiles first before we even arrived at the death chambers. These are the chambers of death and resurrection, because they contain the portals into what the Buddhist path calls the Bardos[9] or the seven hells. In Egypt it was called the death of the seven egos. When the initiate entered those chambers, the sarcophagi were sealed. Almost immediately I felt a sense of being spun downward into the earth, into a specific section of the halls of Amenti[10], where the gates of hell exist. But, you see, what is spoken of as hell in your modern day Bible is a gross misinterpretation. It has incorrectly been made to sound like a place where you are judged by some fear-inducing God, a place you are cast into as punishment for your sins.

These regions of hell, the Bardos, or the seven egos, are simply regions of consciousness. At some point in your spiritual growth, in your process of forgetting and remembering, you have become entrapped in them. You meet nothing in the Bardos that was not totally created by your own ego mind at some point in your lifetime, or lifetimes. When a human being is moving into mastery, he or she must face every addictive temptation, every ego allurement, whether it is for power or for powerlessness in avoidance of responsibility. Whether that ego identity is the victim of rape or incest, or a brutal death, or whether it is a victimizer re-experiencing the horror of the lifetimes in which you have been the one who raped or murdered. If you fear a part of your

---

[8] Editor's note: A book by Amorah Quan Yin, published in 1996, providing a fascinating chronicle of human spiritual evolution from a galactic perspective.

[9] Editor's note: Bardo is a Tibetan word meaning "intermediate state." This refers to the state of existence intermediate between two lives on earth, according to Tibetan Buddhism. The title Bardo Thodol, translated as *The Tibetan Book of the Dead*, actually means: "liberation during the threshold states."

[10] Editor's note: Amenti was depicted as a jackal-headed deity, who stood guard over the city of the dead.

The Tibetan Book of the Dead

Mother Mary, as channeled by Amorah, says: "The regions of hell, the Bardos, are regions of consciousness." This understanding, that at a deep level we make our own reality what it is, is the red thread in *The Tibetan Book of the Dead,* or *Bardo Thodol.*

The text goes back to the 8th century AD, and is traditionally attributed to Padma-Sambhava, an Indian mystic who introduced Buddhism to Tibet. It was written in the Tibetan language and is meant to be a guide for those who have died. There is a legend that Padma-Sambhava, while visiting Tibet, found it necessary to conceal the books he had written. The Tibetans of that time were not ready, so he hid the books in remote locations for them to be discovered at a later time.

The most famous of those who discovered Padma-Sambhava's writings was Karma Lingpa, born around 1350 CE. Karma Lingpa found the hidden text of *The Tibetan Book of the Dead* on top of Mount Gampodar in Tibet when he was fifteen years old. It was first published in English in 1927 by Oxford University Press. Carl Gustav Jung wrote a psychological commentary on the book in 1938.

The *Bardo Thodol* tells how the final moment of the dying process is marked by the sudden appearance of a radiant clear light. This fundamental clear light is identical to a person's mind [is 'mind' the right word?] itself and is said to exist without beginning and continuously through each lifetime and into Buddhahood. For a Buddhist practitioner the nature of the radiant clear light will be immediately recognized and the wisdom necessary for full liberation from the cycle of birth and death will be achieved. Everyone else who fails to recognize the clear light at death will digress into the intermediate state known as the Bardo of Reality, a reality created by mind. The book provides a descriptive map of the bardo experience and also outlines the ritual methods that a lama should employ during the funeral ceremony.
-- *Stephen Muires (editor)*

own psyche, then you are a creator of your own hell. Because if you fear the part of you that has the capacity to be a murderer, you empower it to exist. Whereas if you face it by affirming that there is nothing to be ashamed of, knowing you will never act on this negative ego impulse again and that it is not your truth, then you are free to feel the emotions and transmute them with the power of the Holy Spirit. Then you have true power, because you know you have transcended the capacity for committing harmful acts, or for believing in victimhood. Of course, you would never be asked to go through the test of the Bardos and face your seven egos before you reached a point on your spiritual path at which you have the potential for passing through them successfully. If you are truly moving toward mastery, it is inevitable that you will face this initiation eventually. And yet, when you have truly transcended those false identities and moved beyond guilt, shame, fear, addiction and other ego entrapments, it is no longer a challenge.

When Jesus was eighteen years of age, he and I entered the chambers of death and resurrection together. While in those chambers, we could not submit to a single ego allurement, or judgment, or fear, or shame, or avoidance. If we had reacted with distress to the painful or alluring scenes we witnessed, or even shrunk away, we could not have returned to our bodies. They would have been found dead at the end of the initiation. Remember, the chambers themselves were portals through which we entered into the regions of hell. We could only exit the Bardos by going through them to the other side without believing in or reacting to them. We could not go in reverse. If we had become caught up in and identified with what we witnessed, we would have become entrapped there until we transcended the false identification and released all emotional and mental reactions.

You (Amorah) have something in your psyche to say about this."

Amorah stops channeling and shares what Mother Mary has asked her to share:

When I saw the movie *What Dreams May Come*, I noticed that some people hated the scene about the hells. I sat there in a state of awe the whole time, because I was excited that a movie could be produced that showed people how to go through the Bardos. If the earth would go through a disaster, with a lot of fear and panic, and people were dying, the movie showed people how not to go into the astral planes, simply by not believing in the fear. That is what that movie was doing. It is a

What Dreams May Come

The film from 1998 is based on a 1978 novel by Richard Matheson. Matheson (1926-2013) was a prolific fiction author and screenwriter.  The title of *What Dreams May Come* derives from a line in Hamlet: "For in that sleep of death what dreams may come, when we have shuffled off this mortal coil." The main character in the film is played by Robin Williams (1951-2014).

Amorah points out some of the perceptive experiences in the movie. We have the main character Chris dying in a car accident. The author had done studies of Near Death Experiences and accordingly has Chris meet a guide. Normally this is someone known, a family member that has gone before. In the film the figure is a full-grown Negro man that Chris can only see as a blur initially. Chris asks, "How come I can only see you blurry?" and gets the answer, "Because you don't want to be dead." The guide points out, "We are seeing what we choose to see."

In Amorah's chapter on Transcending Light and Dark, Mother Mary says, "If we had become caught up in and identified with what we witnessed, we would have become entrapped there until we transcended the false identification and released all emotional and mental reactions." This is pretty much exactly what plays out in the movie for the various characters. Chris has to learn to see himself, his relationship, and eventually his children. When he does, he gains freedom.

Annie, Chris's wife, commits suicide and goes to hell. Except, "there are no rules." Hell is presented not as a place of punishment, but as a place of seeing negatively. Annie insists on her own suffering and so her surroundings are hell. The film gives a strong impression of hell, fearful and awful, which was what Amorah noticed when the film came out. Chris realizes, "What's true in our minds, is true." In heaven or hell reality is created by our perception, and the film really brings that point home.
-- *Stephen Muires (editor)*

movie of the times, because it is preparing people to understand that even in the worst circumstances, they can know how to simply look at them and say, "This is not real." With that simple thought, that willingness to not believe in it and identify with it, you can be raised into the light. Mary wanted me to mention that because it is a good modern-day reference point.

Mother Mary continues, "I speak to you of this, because in your daily lives you are in a constant process of preparing yourselves for this final initiation. Even the human beings who do not know about initiations, or the test of the Bardos, are always in a state of preparing themselves, whether they know it or not. When you live in misery, it is because your identity has become engulfed in a hell of your own making. A hell of your own making can also be someone else's hell that you have been repulsed by or afraid of. By having a reaction to someone else's hell, you join them in it. So there exist hell regions that are a co-creation, which are agreed upon as completely as you have all agreed to see the flowers on the table as red. In the same way that you all have agreed to see colors you can agree to see the world as a dangerous place. Or you can choose to see the world as a school that has been created for the purpose of learning the difference between divine truth, relative truth, and illusion. If divine truth is truly ultimate, it will reign supreme eventually.

When your consciousness has explored every other possibility, and has come back home to itself, when your consciousness has recognized that when it had a loving thought free of attachments, good things happened as a result. When your consciousness experiences going through a situation that has been painful in the past with a different attitude, and finds itself not in pain, then you are home.

In the Bardos, in that final initiation, you know you can trust yourself to be a fully sovereign master

> By having a reaction to someone else's hell, you join them in it.

being or Christed one. You will have transcended the need to have mastery over anything other than yourself and your relationship to All That Is. From a practical daily standpoint, think of yourselves as in a constant preparatory test for the Bardos—for you are. In that constant preparation, it is simply an issue of how long your identity stays in a place of pain, addiction and illusion before you return to a place of love, acceptance, and experience of your greatest joy. This is the stuff of which true freedom is made, the stuff of which true self-trust and self-respect are born. This is home, wherever you are.

Namaste."

9 Your Multidimensional Alignment

A channeling from Metatron:

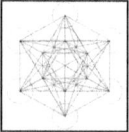

"Your soul's journey through time and space, through dimensions, through levels of reality, through the dream time has been an ongoing movement for most of you for millions of years. There are certain attributes of your own essence, the quality of your being, that have never changed, that have simply become enriched in its understanding of reality on a mental and emotional level. Yet the essence never changes. When you sing the song of the soul that is constantly ringing inside your soul, you are capable of reaching any place in time and dimension to which you have ever been. When you sit in that place of the soul, and you sing that song, you are capable of accessing anything that you have ever experienced.

The only thing that limits your access is your own resistance or fear, or beliefs that are contrary. The soul does not exist within time, even though it has an ability to anchor itself in human consciousness and be in correspondence with the part of you that moves through time.

Your soul is light. Your soul is essence. It is frequency. It is the container of your consciousness that has been used for moving through dimensions and time. The only thing that limits your soul are the false identities that you have taken on during these journeys, that have pulled you from the light into something more solid, something that became fixed for a moment. These places where you became fixed for a moment or for a lifetime or for centuries became like tightness on your timeline. This tightness on your timeline began to impede your consciousness connection to divine source, because part of your negative ego illusion identity has separated it from that place of pure essence.

If in a past lifetime, possibly one in which you were on a higher-dimensional level, you became lost in the illusion of separation, or you became lost in the illusion of low self-worth or victimhood, or lost in any other karmic pattern that was an illusionary product of an experience— if you began to believe that you were that illusion instead of simply the one who experienced it and then moved on, then that part of your consciousness believed it became separate from the innocent place in the soul. The whole spiritual path is simply a process of retrieving those places of misplaced identity of ego and returning them to essence.

Once again, you can be the observer of your reality without being in reaction to it and putting yourself into false consciousness. Feel that connection to the light inside. Imagine that you walked through the days of your life from that place, from that purity, and with everything that happened to you, imagine that you simply witnessed it and sent the soul's light into it. When you met people who were at the same vibration as your soul and had deep experiences with them and noticed that your soul's light became brighter, you might then choose to spend time with those people. They could become life partners or long-term friends. When you were around people who were totally out of touch with their souls, you might find it interesting but you would move on, because there would be no place to communicate from.

As children, you came into the body as a pure being of consciousness and light. For a while you observed what was going on around you. Then you began to identify with what was happening and you began to conclude such things as, "Oooh! People still don't see God; they still don't see the fairies or Jesus or the angels. So if I am going to be here, I had better not see those things either." Or you began to realize that when you were in a place of unconditional love, the people around you would go into fear because they did not know how to handle the frequency. So you decided to match their energy instead of staying in the innocence of your own essence. You didn't know how to stay in a body without something external to relate to.

Then, gradually a persona[11] was developed around all the coping mechanisms for being in the body instead of around the essence of your being. As you had experiences, you thought of them as who you are. You felt victimized by them, or you felt like trying to control them was to your advantage. You believed in the harm as being real, instead of recognizing that what you perceived as harm, or control, or victimhood, or hurt, or limitation, was simply a choice that you made in order to

---

[11] Editor's note: mask or role.

lower your frequency so that you could relate to others, instead of staying in essence. You forgot that you chose it and that you had choices. You even forgot that you had an essence that you could have stayed in. But you chose to separate from it in order to be part of a different reality. Part of the reason for that choice was that every being has certain longings that are inherent to the nature of its soul, that are inherent to the nature of its very beingness. Before you ever became physical human beings, you had experiences in the other dimensions. There you perceived something like separation, you perceived lack of love. You forgot that you had chosen to enter into those realms in order to experience them, because you wanted to know every potential of reality.

Why have you become human? Why have you moved through the dimensions? Why have you played all the roles that you have played? Because you wanted to experience every potential for your beingness. In doing so you began to believe in this separation. You began to believe in the harm instead of witnessing it and moving on to the next experience. The time for self exploration on that level is coming to an end.

You are getting ready to move into the cycle of mastery, in which you begin the process of moving back toward pure essence and back to your true multidimensional self, which has been locked in something

> When you sing the song of the soul, you are capable of reaching any place in time and dimension to which you have ever been.

that is not who you really are. In that ego self you believe that you have lost the connection to the source. In the ego self you are in a false identity.

It is impossible for your essence to ever be separate from source. It is impossible for there to be a moment of existence in which you are not in a sea of love, because it fills everything. It is of such a high frequency that if you are at a frequency lower than that, you cannot feel it.

If your consciousness has become consumed with processing your issues, if your consciousness has become consumed with paranoia around boundary issues, if your consciousness has become consumed with victimhood, then you are locked in a place where the frequency is low enough that you do not feel the connection to divine source. In that place in yourself you feel it is a struggle to survive, because you think of it as All That Is. That part of the ego is struggling to hold onto its position, because it feels that it would die forever if it lost that position. It does not believe in the connection to source.

Go into that place in your soul. Feel it. Feel how simple and quiet it is. Feel how innocent and pure and free of agendas that place is. From that place, ask yourself the question, "What do I long for the most?" Then notice what the feelings of the words are. "What do I long for the most?" See if you can feel that part of you that wants to blend with other souls. That is the way of knowing what others experience. Just simply blend with them in total trust. Feel that place that knows and that wants to blend your soul with another soul, because that is how you know each other.

We would like you to be impulsed now. We are going to ask all of the guides of light who are with us to work with you and your higher self. We would like you to request of us that we begin to impulse you with what it is that keeps you from feeling the innocence of that Oneness with other souls. We want to impulse you to feel what blocks you from that, so that you can begin to release your false identity from that feeling place. We will guide you through a clearing process in order to do so.

I would like you, from the place inside your heart and soul to welcome a Chamber of Light for clearing the blocks that prevent you from feeling your soul essence as your consciousness. As you breathe deeply, we would like you to ask, "What is the primary source of separation from soul in my body consciousness? Let me feel what the energy, the thought, the emotion, the attitude is. What is it in me that is primary in keeping me from feeling my own essence?" Feel what that misplaced consciousness is. Notice where it is in your body. It could be anywhere. At first, just feel it without trying to analyze it; just feel it. Let yourself go in and just feel that energy. Then ask for words to be put to that feeling. You will notice there are some contractions that correspond with the feelings, somewhere in your body. Now ask for the words that go with it. Let that part of you speak its reality, even though you know it is an illusion. Let it speak its reality, so you are very familiar with what it is saying and feeling and where it contracts in your body.

Note that if you took your own consciousness back in time to your very first experience of separation, then there would be some element of that in your body and feelings now. It turns up in your life using different words, but the frequency is very similar.

I would like you now to take the words that you heard and put them in the form of something that you have believed in. Maybe you believed that people would be mad at you all the time if you were in your essence. Maybe you believed that you would find that you still were not good enough if you were in your essence. Maybe you believed someone would try to kill you. Find the words that go along with whatever that belief is for you. Put it into a phrase and understand that this is a picture or symbol.

Now I want you to imagine that picture or symbol attached to your timeline, connected through all of your existence through all of time. I want you to ask that it is cleared everywhere back through your entire timeline, as you cancel it and as you tear it up and burn it. Ask the guides who are here with you to erase any and all pain in your body or on your timeline or in your past lives, pain that is connected with this issue that you are ready to let go of at this time.

We are going to do a clearing of it now, so breathe deeply. Ask that it be cleared through time and space, that all the pain connected to it through time in all your bodies in all dimensions be erased, anything that you are ready to let go of. Tell the guides, "I know that it is time to be done with believing in this. It has controlled me long enough. I am ready to let that ego illusion consciousness go."

Send a message out to divine source, the Holy Mother and Holy Father, to help you from their end, sending their love through your timeline. Your consciousness is sealing the energy from your third dimensional end; theirs is sealing it from the far end. Finally, I would like you to take the picture or symbol now and ask Archangel Michael to hold out his sword of truth. Use the sword of truth to cut through that belief. Say, "This is not my truth." Cut it up and then burn it in a big Rainbow Flame bonfire. The Rainbow Flames can clear on all the energy body levels.

While that clearing continues, ask the guides to impulse you to feel the next place of contraction and give you the words that go with it that keep you from being in divine source and essence connection. There may be different phrases, various distracting voices or distractions you have used to keep from being in source or essence. Ask to feel the next issue that is most key for you at this time. When you feel it, notice where you feel the contraction in your body and the emotions attached to it. Listen to the words. Let it speak all the words that go with that feeling. There may be several phrases. When you feel you have heard all the words, summarize it and do the process we gave you earlier once more until it is clearly released.

Any level of self-importance, any beliefs that you have attached to it, any contracts you have made with yourself to never trust anyone again or to never take risk again or to never let anyone see who you are, any of the contracts you have made with your own self because of false identities—now it is time for them to go. As you find them by going through your own process of clearing them, you can ask for help from us to clear them on your timeline through all lives, through all dimensions. If you are sincerely ready to not believe in them when they come up, the level of release can be very, very far reaching. But if you have been afraid to fully believe in love and have made yourself believe that it was not safe to do so, it is a requirement now that you are willing to let that go. If you promised yourself you would never let go of all the fear, because it would help you stay on guard and not make the same mistakes again, then you have to be willing to let it go.

Understand that these fears are false identities. Even though they are also coping mechanisms, they came into being because you did not believe in your connection to divine source when you created the coping mechanism. You are capable of once again believing in your connection to divine source. If you are willing.

Ask Sekhmet[12], a goddess of light, to help you see yourself. Ask to see where your identity has been misplaced and where these coping mechanisms have kept you from your true soul, from the divine source and essence connection. Ask the guides to give you the courage to be willing to feel any fear or emotion attached to them, so you can go beyond them. So that you can be the Christed One embodied. So that you can be the one who again lives in that state of innocence and love and trust that is who you really are.

We thank you for the depth of your willingness to go into this experience and into the place of truth with yourself. Now you can call on me and on others of the light. Know that when we look to the future, we see a great celebration and a great victory. Know that you are a part of that victory. Know that the courage and the strength that you are gaining through moving through these issues and to live in truth this time, has great rewards. Know that who you are on an essence level is worthy. Know that you have never been flawed and that there has never been a moment when you were a disappointment to the Holy

---

[12] Editor's note: Sekhmet is an Egyptian goddess of both destruction and of healing. Her name means "the powerful one." She is depicted as a lioness. It is said that her fire breath created the desert.

Mother and Holy Father and that there has never been a moment in which you were truly harmed. There has never been a moment in all of existence in which you were not loved unconditionally.

In the spirit of Oneness and the spirit of the light and love and innocence and beauty of All That Is, so la re en lo[13]."

— Metatron

[Amorah continues:] As a way of renewing your divine connection to All That Is, I want to guide you through a process for connecting deeply to your true multidimensional self. We will be doing this connecting process on several higher-dimensional levels, starting with your Christ conscious self of the fourth, fifth, and sixth dimensions. The Christ conscious self is in appearance between 10 and 12 feet tall; roughly twice your body's height.

Second comes the part of you that is seventh and eighth dimensional, which happens to be the level of Melchizedek, Christ's teacher. Your seventh and eight dimensional self is between 30 and 34 feet tall, or about five times as tall as you are.

The third level of connection goes to the ninth and tenth dimensional level of consciousness, which is also the level of Metatron, or Melchizedek's teacher. This dimensional self is about 60 to 70 feet tall.

Last are the eleventh and twelfth dimensional levels which are the realms of Lords, Archangels and Elohim. On the upper level you will have a connection to one of these, but not to all three. Even if you are unsure of the realm, you can still make the connection. This part of you has a height that is infinite.

Let us do that process now.

Connecting to your true multidimensional self[14]

1. First, make a deep higher self light connection as shown in *The Pleiadian Workbook: Awakening You Divine Ka.*

2. Ask for Archangel Michael to be with you holding his sword of truth as divine protection.

---

[13] Editor's note: "So it is, so be it," in the Pleiadian language.
[14] Editor's note: an earlier version of this exercise can also be found in *The Pleiadian Tantric Workbook: Awakening Your Divine Ba.*

∞

3. Now visualize a diamond light infinity symbol going through your first, or root, chakra up to the root chakra of your Christed self. Then connect that infinity symbol to your seventh and eighth dimensional root chakra. Then to your ninth and tenth dimensional self's root chakra. And finally to your eleventh and twelfth dimensional self's root chakra. Breathe deeply to feel each of these links as you make them.

4. Next visualize a diamond light infinity symbol going through your second chakra up to the second chakra of your Christed self. Then connect that infinity symbol to your seventh and eighth dimensional second chakra. Then to your ninth and tenth dimensional self's second chakra. And finally to your eleventh and twelfth dimensional self's second chakra. Breathe deeply to feel each of these links as you make them.

5. Now visualize a diamond light infinity symbol going through your third chakra up to the third chakra of your Christed self. Then connect that infinity symbol to your seventh and eighth dimensional third chakra. Then to your ninth and tenth dimensional self's third chakra. And finally to your eleventh and twelfth dimensional self's third chakra. Breathe deeply to feel each of these links as you make them.

6. Next visualize a diamond light infinity symbol going through your heart chakra up to the heart chakra of your Christed self. Then connect that infinity symbol to your seventh and eighth dimensional heart chakra. Then to your ninth and tenth dimensional self's heart chakra. And finally to your eleventh and twelfth dimensional self's heart chakra. Breathe deeply to feel each of these links as you make them.

7. Visualize a diamond light infinity symbol going through your throat chakra up to the throat chakra of your Christed self. Then connect that infinity symbol to your seventh and eighth dimensional throat chakra. Then to your ninth and tenth dimensional self's throat chakra. And finally to your eleventh and twelfth dimensional self's throat chakra. Breathe deeply to feel each of these links as you make them.

8. Next visualize a diamond light infinity symbol going through your sixth, or third eye chakra up to the third eye chakra of your Christed self. Then connect that infinity symbol to your seventh and eighth dimensional third eye chakra. Then to your ninth and tenth dimensional self's third eye chakra. And finally to your eleventh and twelfth dimensional self's third eye chakra. Breathe deeply to feel each of these links as you make them.

9. Finally, visualize a diamond light infinity symbol going through your crown chakra up to the crown chakra of your Christed self. Then connect that infinity symbol to your seventh and eighth dimensional crown chakra. Then to your ninth and tenth dimensional self's crown chakra. And finally to your eleventh and twelfth dimensional self's crown chakra. Breathe deeply to feel each of these links as you make them.

10. Just relax and enjoy this deep connection as long as you would like.

You can do this meditation as often as you would like. Repetition will deepen the connection and gradually make it more permanent as you do it. Enjoy!

10 Sovereignty

Sovereignty means that you are your own ruler or master. There is no one above you. You only answer to yourself. We are all sovereign beings of light that are equal. You do not need a guru or anyone to tell you what to do. You have it all inside yourself. Whatever you choose, you are the chooser.

At this special time on earth we are moving toward our mastery and full enlightenment. You do not get there by relying on others. Can you imagine being at "heaven's gate" and being asked why you should get in? You reply, "Well, I was a disciple of _____ and I did everything he/she told me to." I think they would say, "Rejected. Go back."

Many people have this type of co-dependent reliance on others. It could be a marriage partner, a guru, a spiritual teacher, someone who wrote a book, a close friend.

> You do not need a guru to tell you what to do.

These people do not trust their inner knowing and they live in self-doubt and irresponsibility. They always try to do what others say or recommend, so they do not have to become self-reliant. But how can you become enlightened and move toward mastery that way? Mastery means that you have become the master unto yourself, with no superiors. Mastery is sovereignty in action 24/7.

If you live in a way that makes you give away authority to others, you are still the chooser. It is a very bad choice. You are here to learn to actively become your own master in everything. All answers you need are inside you. All of them. You may learn from a spiritual teacher, healer or author. You may learn from a partner or friend. Yet you choose what you believe. You are the chooser even if you choose to give your power away.

Power is not an issue about controlling other people or situations. It is about being in you inner power and trusting yourself and your inner guidance. However, if you never allow yourself to follow inner guidance and you never trust yourself, you are the one who chooses that. You are still the master over your destiny, no matter whether you choose wisely or from the negative ego self. Even if you choose to follow someone else, you are one who chooses. No one else ever controls your life and your choices. Only you do.

What a glorious reality. You are the master of your fate whether you realize it or not! If you do not speak your truth, you make that choice. Someone else may try to intimidate you or make you afraid, but you are the one who chooses to allow this to be your reality. It does not ever matter what another person does. It matters only whether you allow that to control your life or not. Even if you choose to let them choose, you are still the one who chose to allow that to happen.

If you have people in your life like that, clear all contracts with them now. Make a new commitment to yourself to move into your spiritual mastery. Become the conscious ruler of your own life and fate.

A good place to start is with meditation and higher-self connection. Learning to ground and be in your body is a good beginning. You can learn these processes from *The Pleiadian Workbook*, which I wrote. After you have begun grounding and doing the higher self connection, start practicing becoming the observer or watcher during meditation.

Becoming the watcher during meditation is a great way to learn more about yourself. What does your ego personality do to try to distract you? Do not judge it, just observe and consciously choose. Being the watcher or observer is a path toward finding your true self. You are a beautiful being of light moving through life like a student in school. Everything is a lesson. When you see this, you start to move out of the "robotic mentality" and move back to who you really are.

You already are a sovereign master of your own destiny. You may simply have been using that truth haphazardly. Stop and assess yourself and your life choices. Do you move through your days in an automatic way that you have become programmed to do? Do you respond to life in trust and presence, or do you respond as an automaton doing what it is "supposed to do?" Do you consciously choose what you are doing? Or are you the robot? Do you have enough presence with yourself to consciously observe what happens in life, or do you simply always fit in?

Many people made contracts with themselves as children or with their parents, that they must try to be like everyone around them and hide their true self. Are you like that? If you are, clear those contracts and make a new pledge to yourself to begin to question the reality you live in and your own choices within that reality. As you meditate regularly you can begin to become more present with yourself, with other people, and with life circumstances. As you become more present you start to sense your inner guidance more easily.

The guides and higher self are not here to do it for you. They are here to help you own your sovereignty and move into conscious mastery. They understand that if they try to do it for you, you will never learn to do it for yourself. A true guide of light or higher self will often ask you questions. They are there to help you learn to think things through in your own unique way. They want you to weigh the pros and cons and choose to do what is absolutely the best and most right thing.

One of the ways of life that this leads to is you breaking through and always speaking your truth, never holding back with anyone for any reason. If you agree with someone, you say you do. If you do not agree with someone, you say that also. If you are not being treated in a respectful way by someone, you tell them how that makes you feel and ask them why they are doing it. If this leads to a big eruption from them, then so be it. You are not responsible for their reaction. You are only responsible for speaking your truth.

Years ago I had an experience of this type of situation with a woman. I was at her house and she started talking about her housemate in a very angry and judgmental way. I interrupted her and told her I would prefer not to continue the conversation, because I had made a commitment in life to being nonjudgmental. I told her I realized how much our being judgmental has the ability to harm someone. She turned on me in a nasty way and said, "I have good reasons for feeling this way." I said, "If you want to share your feelings, I will be a sounding board, but I will not listen to you trashing this person." I left very soon after that, as it became obvious she was unwilling to hear what I was saying and would continue in this negative way.

I personally believe that when we make commitments to ourselves of this nature, we always have to live up to them. When someone else is not, we can tell them our choices and why. If they still do not wish to comprehend and get it, we can always speak our truth and walk away. In order to do this we must be at a place inside ourselves to not take things personally.

Everyone in the world is learning and growing at their own rate.

You may be farther ahead in certain areas and farther behind in others. When we see that this is the truth, we can learn that nothing anyone ever does has anything to do with us, not really. They live in an expression of where they are in their own growth and evolution. If they still practice being judgmental, dishonest or anything else that is undesirable, they would do it with anyone that happens to be around. It has nothing to do with you. You just happen to be there, instead of someone else. Therefore, even if it seems like a personal affront, it is not. It is just them living in their current state of understanding and growth. Love and compassion are the natural things to feel when you understand this.

Love and compassion are the natural way of being for someone who is sovereign. The sovereign spiritual master has learned that it is not his/her job to rule over others. His/her job is to honor the universal law of free will. We are responsible for always following that law. We can never send a healing to someone who does not want it and who does not approve of it. We can never try to teach something to a person who does not want to learn. Proselytizing is a breach of the law of free will. We can defend ourselves and speak our truth. However, if someone says they do not want to hear it, we are bound to walk away and no longer engage. It is possible to walk away in a loving and compassionate way that is free of judgment. Always know that the other person has a universal right to be exactly where they are with their life in this earth school.

To be a true sovereign is to rely on yourself and your inner knowing in a deep and honest way. By embodying all of the positive qualities this book is about, you can do that. Trust that your inner guidance is there, even if you have not yet become aware of it. You will. It is inevitable.

Part 4

Home

in

Oneness

11 Invincibility of Spirit

Coming home to ourselves involves every dimensional level: emotional, mental, physical, and spiritual. It does not matter whether we are from Andromeda, another universe, Sirius, or the Pleiades. Where we are is home, no matter the physical location.

In this new age, people sometimes say, "I don't belong here. We don't operate this way on the planet I come from." Believe me, we did not end up here by accident. We are here because we chose to be here, on a planet where we are learning to live in what seems like a limited reality. We are here because we are learning that home is totally a product of consciousness.

When we learn to be home here, we recognize that we may never go back to where we came from. If the whole spiritual growth and learning process is linear in the long run, then we will never return. We will always be moving forward. Being at home is the ability to totally let go of the past with a snap of a finger and to move on without looking back. Home is when you are present with yourself.

At some point in the past, the Elohim started working with us by helping our cells to spin properly so that we could return to what they call the "matrix of divine flow." When we are in that divine flow, we are home wherever we are, even in our cellular structures which have greatly been mutated over eons. The Elohim took us on two different journeys, with the Mer people and the Lemurian energies, to help us remember how to bring the divine into the body. In Lemuria there was a time when our bodies were freshly created and there was no cellular mutation. We worked with Lemurian energies to re-anchor our memory of what it is like to be in a non-mutated form. From there we examined the attitudes that we need to have in order to not feel separate, in order to create home within.

We explored how often we create the illusion of separation

through our attitudes of distrust, living in suspicion and living in fear of something going wrong. These attitudes keep us in a level of contraction, so we never feel fully at home wherever we are. Ironically, the motivation behind the attitudes is a deep desire in all of us to feel at home, comfortable, and peaceful. However, because our approach contains fear, we live in fear. Not all the time, but in subtle ways such as when we tense or contract when we see someone doing something we do not like. We try to protect ourselves by shutting down. It does not work, because what we have actually done has created separation. In that contraction, we have blocked the natural way of spirit to radiate and flow.

A whale energy came in once and filled the whole room. It was chanting "home." Think of the word. There is sacredness in the English language. 'Ho' is saying yes in the Native American language; it is an affirmation: 'Ho.' Followed by 'om,' which is the sound of God. Together it is saying, yes to the sound of God. In singing 'home,' we are saying yes to our god selves. We are affirming that is who we are.

Perfection in all that exists springs from divine source. The eternal life that is in every consciousness that has ever become aware of its own existence springs from divine source. In divine source, there is only home, there is only Oneness, there is only you.

When your connection to divine source has become an ineffable process and part of your daily life, something undisputable and invincible has happened. You are here to share the spirit of invincibility. You are here to share the spirit of divine flow from source into All That Is.

Take a deep breath and ask yourself this question: What would it mean to want nothing more than this moment? Notice what you feel in your body when you ask yourself that question. Breathe into every cell. What would it mean to want nothing but this moment, and to know that the past has been blessed and the next moment will take care of itself?

You come closest to that way of living when you talk about the meditative state of 'no mind.' The meditative state of 'no mind' means being present and having no mental agenda. This means that even if you have a great vision, the moment it is gone, it is gone. You simply remain in presence. Presence is what is invincible. Presence is being present with the thought that applies to the moment. Presence is being present with the silence, with no thought of the moment. Presence is the witnessing of the one who sits before you or the one that basks in aloneness.

Even if you have goals, the invincibility of divine presence is knowing when to ponder a goal and its perfection, and when to simply release it, because it is no longer needed. Presence requires non-attachment. Invincibility can only live in detachment. These are words you have heard so many times, 'detachment' and 'attachment,' and yet they are often formed and apprehended on the mental plane. The great need of true seekers for home is to *feel* the quality of non-attachment. To have a concept of being unattached is beautiful, but unless the feeling of non-attachment flows from it, it is useless. The only purpose is to stimulate right action, feeling, and presence.

On the spiritual quest, nothing is required of you beyond what you, as your true self, require of you. When you come back to reenact a karmic pattern, it is because your

> The only way your invincibility
> is threatened is by believing
> that it is not choice.

own spirit has longed to do it again, but in a more correct way. When you return into another life to reconnect with an old karmic partner and work out the flaws in the relationship, it is a gift you have given to yourselves. Sometimes that gift has been somewhat ego-polluted, so to speak, although that is part of the learning as well. Sometimes you choose to do it out of guilt, or shame, or the feeling that you must serve penitence, or because you want revenge. All of these things certainly bind you to the negative aspect of the karmic path, but you did not come here for those reasons. You came here to transcend them.

When you leave here, it will be because you have released those reasons and have simply done enough. Ultimately, you will not leave here because you need to; you will leave here when you are finished. The need to leave the earth plane is one of the things that binds you to it, because your own spirit demands that you live in non-avoidance in order to feel the limitlessness of every level of reality. If you are in such a hurry to get out of this hell hole, then you will live in dread of it, even in the higher dimensions. Even there, in the higher dimensions, everything is not as crystal clear as you think it is. We still feel those things that we have left undone and send our love to them. We honor the perfection of All That Is, and sometimes your higher self wants to come back one more time just to see what it would feel like to do it this way. All the ideas of victimhood and being stuck here are absolutely not the way it is. Many of the karmas that you reenact are simply because you have chosen to do so.

Your invincibility is not threatened by anything you choose to do. The only way your invincibility is threatened is by believing that it is not choice. The only way your invincibility is ever threatened is by believing that something was done to you against your will. There is never an instant in your life that is not a mirror on some level. Even if something happens to you because you did not choose otherwise. Maybe you did not directly create it, but you nevertheless did not create something else. There is learning in that.

Invincibility is a product of gratefully accepting responsibility for everything that has ever been and ever shall be in your consciousness and in your life. When your consciousness is aligned with divine source and truth, there is nothing that can be done to you that can cause damage. We know this sounds impossible. Although Christians have somewhat misused the story of Christ on the cross, it is nevertheless a great example of how a soul cannot be damaged if that soul stays aligned with higher purpose. You may feel pain, but you, as an essence being of light, cannot be harmed. In your psyche you have somehow twisted together the idea of harm with physical reality, and thus you have in many ways limited yourself and become a victim in your own life. It is just like in the words of this simple song: "You can choose what you see. You can choose."

If a person stands before you with a gun pointed at your head, you can choose to see him or her as a being of light who has forgotten what he or she is. You can choose to have compassion for that being instead of feeling sorry for yourself. Do not feel guilty because you do not do this at all time. I simply wish to impress you with an energy to which you can aspire, and maybe you do live there already. There is never a moment, when a person pulls out in front of you in their car, or someone at a cash register is throwing off anger, when you need to think: "What an angry person, throwing all those darts!" That is a waste of spirit energy. You destroy your own invincibility the moment you have the thought. The only thing that is needed is to see that beautiful being of light before you and observe with your discernment. Perhaps you need to have boundaries in that moment, but the only boundary you actually need is to love the person. If you radiate love, there is no place for the darts to stick. If you contract in opposition to them, then you become your own victimizer. Your contraction creates the harm you feel. If you choose to love, you are invincible.

To strive for invincibility is to say: "Every day of my life, I am so grateful. I can choose to cancel every thought that is a waste of energy and threatens my invincibility and the invincibility of other people." In truth you cannot harm another person's invincibility, but you can contribute to the size of the illusion they have created that masks it. It is rather a paradox. There is co-creation, but when you become conscious of yourself as the creator of your own reality, no one can affect your invincibility except you. The moment you give power to a thought that limits yourself, you have limited your own invincibility.

If you realize you feel angry, ashamed, or fearful, thank yourself for the awareness that those emotions are there. Now you know what to clear from yourself, what part of you needs love the most. When you love that part of yourself, instead of being ashamed or resentful that you still have inner work to do, you can stay invincible even in the process of restoring invincibility.

Whether you respond with gratitude or with judgment to each moment in life determines your invincibility versus your imprisonment, invincibility or harm. Only you have the capacity to harm yourself, even with a thought. If someone hurls at you the most horrible insult you can imagine, you can be invincible if you do not take it personally. Taking it personally would let it into you. If you receive it, you can choose to be hurt by it. In that moment you diminish your invincibility temporarily, because part of your consciousness has become locked in illusion. Where your consciousness is, that is where your home is in this moment.

The following is a process from the realm of Metatron to receive the frequency of the invincibility of spirit:

Receive the invincibility of spirit

1. Come into your heart and into your presence.

2. Welcome one of the angels of Metatron and/or one of the Elohim.

3. Put your hands out, palms up.

4. Ask the angel of Metatron or the Elohim to come and take your hands. Breathe deeply as you welcome the connection. Be very aware

of your feeling at this time, because it is through feeling that you will be able to receive what you are being given.

5. Take a deep breath.

6. Imagine that you can look directly into the eyes of your guide and say to the guide: "I am invincible."

7. Scan your body and notice what you feel. Do you feel ashamed? Do you feel urgent? Do you feel peaceful and present?

8. Now say it aloud: "I am invincible." Be sure that when you say it, you are saying it to your body. Notice the feeling that is stimulated.

9. Now change the affirmation slightly. Say: "I am ready for invincibility of spirit."

10. Notice if any place in your body contracts. Notice if you feel shame, anger, joy, love, or quiet.

11. You may notice a presence coming in, around, and above the room now. This is an aspect of your own future self all the way from the Great Central Sun from that time in your future when you are so fully reconnected to your true self and source that you know invincibility without doubt. If you feel a joyful, childlike, innocent, wise being around you, know that it is you.

12. Welcome your own future self now to take one of your hands as your guide continues to hold the other.

13. Do the affirmation again adding the word 'now': "I am ready for invincibility of spirit, now." Notice if there is any part of you at all that cringes away from believing it and is afraid to hope.

14. Breathe and notice what you feel, as you consider the following questions: What if invincibility of spirit meant letting go of your most cherished future plan? What if it meant that the thing you have aspired to the most is not necessary, that just aspiring to it is enough? What if you were told that it was time for you to end being in a relationship now? What if it was time for you to enter into relationships now? What

would you feel if you were told that what you want most is not necessary for your path anymore? Breathe, and feel, and relax your shoulders.

15. If there is part of you that is a little disturbed, tell it that everything is okay. Affirm: "I am ready for invincibility of spirit—now." Breathe and feel it.

16. Look at your hands and say: "The power of invincibility lies in my own hands."

17. Take a deep breath and notice what you really feel in your body.

18. Now say: "I trust myself to use invincibility wisely." Notice what you feel.

19. Shake hands with yourself and say: "I agree to use the power of invincibility wisely." Breathe and feel. Do you believe yourself? If you do not, it is okay, because you have learned you need to work on self-trust, and you can do that.

20. Take another deep breath all the way through your body.

21. Give permission to the Metatron angels to begin a laser alignment of your energy centers to help heal the communication between your chakras, your body, your spirit, your emotions, and your consciousness. Receive laser-like streams of energy into your chakras from above, in front and behind. If you feel that something is being lifted above you, simply breathe and assist the lifting. Cellular, genetic and thought-form energies that limit you and from which you have already learned your lessons are being lifted. Just allow the lifting in grace. Breathe deeply but gently and allow five minutes of silence for the alignment.
    The laser alignment will be followed by a light activation that will continue for 24 hours.

22. Ask the Metatron angels to blend with your energy field now to raise your frequency and do a healing and strengthening of your Pillar of Light alignment through the higher dimensions. Let your mouth be open a little.

23. Think of yourself as a diamond of perfection: pure, clear, perfectly cut and filled with light. You now receive streams of light-encoded fibers from the Elohim to help restore the fibers of light in your sacred geometry and in your etheric, physical, emotional, mental, and spiritual bodies. Welcome this cocooning or down stepping of light encodings and hold the attitude of willingness to let go of every illusion that blocks you from seeing and experiencing that diamond perfection: invincibility.

24. Affirm: "I am willing now to be the perfection that I am."

25. Affirm: "I am the perfection that I am."

26. Breathe. Ask yourself: "Do I believe it?" If part of you does not, then send it love.

27. Consider the following: are you ready to release getting attention through complaining? Are you ready to let go of the self-importance that comes from suffering or from being the one who always tries harder than anyone else? Are you ready to celebrate that everyone else is as bright a light as you are and not feel dimmed by that?

28. Affirm: "I choose to embrace the power of invincibility now."

29. Breathe deeply. If there is a place inside you that is still holding on to pain and resistance, focus your love there and silently ask the guides to come. They will help you to release it by sending the appropriate laser energy to assist you and your love.

The invincibility of you as a spirit embodied is a state that you can achieve now and always. When there is nothing at all inside of you that is negative and illusionary, negative energy cannot stick to you. When your higher self has become fully embodied into your third dimensional self, illusionary negative energy cannot stick to you. Applying the teachings up until now in this book can actually assist you in your process of becoming invincible. You are that invincibility if you choose it consciously.

12 Unity in Diversity

Unity in diversity is the main goal of what we are here on earth to achieve. It means we learn to live with everything and everyone exactly as they are, in complete love, no matter how different they are from us. No matter what religion, race, color, creed or level of spiritual evolution, we simply choose to accept them and unconditionally love them exactly as they are, free of the need to change them into who we think they should be.

What things do we have to practice in our lives in order to embrace unity in diversity? Being nonjudgmental, no blame for anything, no belief in betrayal, no illusions of limitation and, of course, living in invincibility as our true selves. Can we do this? Of course we can. That is why we are here.

A meditation for releasing blockages to unity in diversity

1. Breathe deeply and focus on being present in your body.
(When you contract and hold constriction of any kind in your body, your cells are not able to spin properly and send their light out. You draw astral energies to yourself with your contraction. One of the ways of knowing the difference between when you are in spirit and when you are in ego, is to ask the following: "Am I contracted or am I radiating when I have this thought?" Ego energies tend to suppress the light. They may be old fears, judgments, or pity.)

2. Breathe deeply and tell your body that you have an intention of learning how to be open and flowing. Give yourself permission to open and let go.

3. Welcome the Dolphin Star Temple Higher Council of Light.

4. Ask that the City of Light be anchored in the room or environment where you are now.

5. Ask your higher self of the light to stand in front of you and to appear in a full body form. It might look angelic, fairy-like, or whatever it chooses.

6. Hold your hands palms facing out. Ask your higher self to come now and place the palms of its hands on yours.

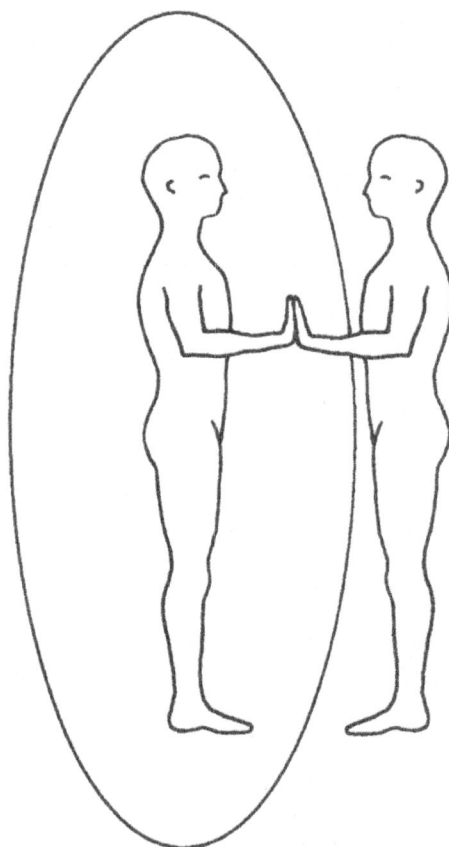

7. Focus on breathing in through your hands and allowing the energy being sent from your own divine higher self to move into your arms.

8. Breathe the energy up through your arms into your heart. As your heart fills, let the energy spread through your body from there.

9. Imagine that you can look deeply into the eyes of your higher self.

10. Ask your higher self if it has a name it would like you to use when you call it in. Understand that sometimes they prefer no name.

11. Blend with your higher self. The following is a process for bringing your higher self into your body as much as you can at this time, to become the divine One:
(One of the goals for many of us on the spiritual path is to come to the point where there is no higher self to call in because it is grounded through the body all the time. Our consciousness is the divine self. If you have tended to think of the higher self as a higher aspect of yourself, you might stop to realize that you are just a smaller aspect of it. It is the other way around: the human self is just a little piece of the I Am Presence. In this meditation, you are saying that you want to be in contact with all of your I Am Presence, all of your higher consciousness.)

12. Take a minute or so of silence to feel the connection of the higher self in your physical body. Realize that the divine energy you are feeling is you. It is what you really are.

13. Ask your higher self to stay blended with you in your body throughout the next phase of this meditation and the visualization work.

14. Think about the last time you judged someone. You had a thought like: "How did he do such a stupid thing?" or "What an arrogant guy or woman!" or any thought that in any way diminished another person. Include times when you were impatient with someone, because impatience is also a judgment.

15. As you start to remember, feel where in your body you contracted when you judged that person. You will notice that the light begins to dim. Ask your higher self to stay while you are feeling this. As you remember your experience, consider: What did you feel when that happened? Where did you contract? Where did your identity go? Who were you in that moment? Of course, it is part of your negative ego in

those moments of judging, but do not judge yourself; that is just more ego. The trick is to make a new choice.

16. Take a deep breath and let go of the memory.

17. Take another deep breath and feel your higher self connection.

18. Ask your higher self to help you replace that experience with how you would have responded in the situation if you had been in your higher self identity, instead of your lower ego identity. Again, this is not to judge; it is practicing living in a sacred way. You practice responding from higher self consciousness with love. Notice the difference in what happens in your body and your breath.

19. Ask your higher self to fill those places in your body where you tend to hold judgment and contraction. Ask your higher self to take over and fill those places with its light.

20. Ask the guides who are present to assist you now in sending a little ball of violet flame to the person that you judged or were impatient with. Have this flame go to the person and dissolve the energy that you sent to them when you judged them.

When you indulge in believing in a negative thought about someone, you send them a harmful energy, because thought is energy in motion. Send the violet flame out with the intention of dissolving and transmuting the energy that you used in a hurtful way. Even if you are not consciously thinking about hurling energy at someone and hurting them, if you do not cancel the thought, that is what happens.

21. Now take a moment to forgive yourself for not canceling the judgment at the time it occurred.

22. Make a plan that you will catch the thought sooner and cancel it the next time you judge. If it is in your heart to do so, ask your higher self to help you be benevolent in your thoughts and attitudes toward yourself and others.

23. Take a deep breath. Open your eyes now, and come back to the room.

There is a process called the Matrix of Divine Flow[15]. It has to do with getting your cells to correct their spin patterns and move in the rhythms of creation. In order to have this healing, this un-mutating of your cellular structure, there are five basic qualities that must be held. These allow for the Elohim and the angels of grace to assist you in correcting the flow patterns. When you are out of sync and your chakras are not working right, when your cells are spinning sluggishly, it is because the frequency of your thoughts and your emotions have slowed them down and made them mutate. The Elohim say you can correct that and heal every issue if you live in five qualities all the time.

The first quality is referred to as the 'ground that you plant seeds in': it is basic self-acceptance. If that is 100% your intention, and you can embrace that intention even when the lack of self-acceptance comes up—it is enough. Intention draws energy too. Self-acceptance is the basic groundwork. The second quality is divine love that is unconditional and free of attachment. The third quality is divine trust that is free of distrust and contraction, and that uses discernment. The fourth quality is unity in diversity, the acceptance without separation, judgment, and prejudice of other peoples' differences, no matter what they are. The fifth quality is surrender to divine will, which is basically doing what you know is absolutely the right thing to do.

In those times on the earth when the mystery schools were part of society, people who were indulging in lower frequencies would not be allowed into them. This was the case not just in Egypt but also in any culture—including the Native Americans' when they shared shamanic teachings and gave initiations. These systems knew that it was unwise to give people information that they could not handle properly.

Most of our culture is not capable of comprehending what it takes to live in unity in diversity and divine trust, much less divine love. To embrace unity in diversity and divine trust means we have to assume innocence on the part of other people. Not in a naive way, but we do need to assume innocence. Even if the action on the part of the person is not innocent, we need to trust that they still have a part of themselves that is innocent, and we need not blame them for being out of touch with it at that moment. If we are blamed for every moment in which we are not in touch with our innocence and not acting from innocence, it would be a very heavy sentence. It would be like living as a suspect all the time.

---

[15] Editor's note: this process can be found in Amorah's book *Affinity*, chapter 27.

I have become aware that we in our culture do live in suspicion most of the time. We are on the lookout for when people are going to screw up. We are even more ready to catch the people who we really love or the people who really offer good things to us, because we keep thinking something has to be wrong. We may not consciously be thinking these things, but there is an energy that is flowing and waiting for something to hook onto. "I should have known better than to trust them." It is as if a part of us is waiting to say those words. We are inundated in our culture with the idea that things are too good to be true, that there is no one that you can trust, and that you need to be on guard and hold yourself back all the time in preparation for it, because if you are not on guard, you will be caught off guard, and that is the worst. Basically we walk around thinking, "You're suspect. You're suspect." We literally live in a state of distrust and expect the worst from people.

The energy of trust is so important. The guides have told me that, even if a person is a liar and thief, for you to sit around in distrust, scrutiny, and suspicion about that person is for you to hold on to the idea of separation and the illusion of judgment. You do not have to do that to use discernment. If you trust yourself to be aware of what is going on, then you do not have to stop flowing love and light for a moment. You do not have to judge yourself when you are suspicious or reactive. Instead, when you catch it, clear it, and come back to your higher truth as soon as possible.

If you need to process emotions, call in the guides. I realize that this is something some people do not know. Some people tighten up when their emotions are moving, because they do not want to shoot them out at people. They do not realize that as they tighten up, they are drawing the person that they are thinking about into them. When your energy is focused on someone, the moment you start contracting to hold the emotion in, you draw the person in psychically. And you shoot out cords to them, because a thought has not been released through the higher levels. You need to move the energy of the emotion up through your chakras to transmute it, not repress it because it is a lower thought or emotion. Transmute the emotion in a way that is safe for you and the other person. For example, this simply means to acknowledge, "I feel anger. It's not my truth." Then surround yourself with rainbow flames, or ask St. Germaine to hold the violet flame around you, or ask Archangel Michael to seal the space with his sword of truth. Whichever master or archangel you work with, call on them and tell them you need to let the anger go, and you do not want to hurt anyone. If it is a quick thought that you can cancel immediately and move into love, you do not have to call them in. When it is something that has gotten hold of you repeatedly, then ask the guides to create a bubble around you so that you can release the energy through your chakras and transmute it. It is not your truth. You do not want to repress it and keep back the light out through repression. You do not want to harm yourself or others with the emotions. You let that energy move.

You have a choice, even when you have a reaction, not to let it be your truth. It is just a reaction, and you can choose to witness and change it. Witnessing is a very basic tool on the spiritual path. It is not much in use in the new age community, because a lot of people have become involved through books and don't have many of the basic teachings.[16]

You can be an example of a chosen way of responding by not indulging your emotions. There is a point on the path where self-indulgence makes the whole path hypocrisy. If you are going to live by doing what you know is right each moment, which is surrender to divine will, then if you know that judgment travels to people, you need to cancel it. You know that wanting to prove to someone that you are right, so that you can prove them wrong, is an issue of negative ego. I do not care how strong the pull is and how much you want to say what you want to say, you instead have the choice to breathe and to refuse to say it, to go process it and cancel it on your own.

Some people think that, in the name of being honest, they are supposed to say everything they feel. Expressing anger to the person they are angry with is an abusive act, because unless they are doing it in a responsible way (which means not going out and attacking someone with it), they are giving power to the lower ego again.

How can we live in this day-to-day world with its frustrations? For me, trying to find something on the Internet brings up my issues of helplessness and being out of control. When that happens, I am therefore choosing to work on the issue instead of sitting, seething, and swearing. Even though it is not a person that I am directing my judgment at, the negative energy is nevertheless going out into the field

---

[16] Editor's note: Witnessing here refers to an honest self-examination and admission of what feelings, emotions and thoughts are moving through oneself. By contrast, in Christianity the term 'witnessing' means a sharing of the faith, of how a person found Jesus, usually for the purpose of evangelizing.

around earth. I do not want to use products that contaminate, and I do not want to send out thoughts that contaminate. I choose to live a life of not doing it, yet I still have this issue come up. It is good to laugh at myself about it and not take it so seriously, yet not take it so lightly that I do not have the sobriety of caring. There is a time and place for sobriety, which is not a contracted seriousness, but a sobriety on the spiritual path that shows that I will do what it takes to live my truth. It does not matter if I am angry and no one knows it. I know it does not work that way. I can be on the moon and my thoughts will still reach the person I am mad at.

When someone approaches you with a certain energy, the natural tendency is to match the frequency of that person. If a person hits you with negative energy, the most natural thing for most humans to do is to respond with defensiveness, which is a contracted energy that matches the attack. Instead of defending, what if all you needed to do was be yourself with nothing to prove? What I have learned to do when someone judges me or attacks me is to feel compassion for the person who considers him or herself on a spiritual path and yet is so suspicious of others that they are waiting to do them wrong or waiting for others to do something stupid. I send a message that Christ asked me to use a long time ago. It is: "Why do you have the need to get angry and assume that I intentionally did something wrong to you?"

In *The Celestine Prophecy* there is a story of a gas station attendant who was very angry toward the two travelers, a man and a woman, who were gathering the prophecies. The man got defensive back and met the attendant's anger tit for tat. The woman intervened and told the man to stop. She said to the attendant, "Why do you have the need to be so angry with us right now?" Because the question was asked from a place of innocence, the attendant stopped and thought about it.

When people come at us with any kind of blame and attack energy, what if we could stay in a loving center and respond in truth without defensiveness? What if we simply responded with what our reality was? If an emotion comes up about it, we do not act upon it. What if we were responsible enough that when someone comes at us with negativity we could stop, take a deep breath and say, "Do you want an answer, or do you want to

> This world has taught us that when things go wrong, somebody is doing something to us.

The Celestine Prophecy

Amorah mentions the novel *The Celestine Prophecy*, focusing on just one scene that highlights a new way of being, a different way of handling emotions.

The book was published in 1993, and made into a film in 2006. James Redfield, the author of the novel, wrote the book during a series of coincidences that inspired the message of the book. This included an occasion of following the flight path of a crow into the canyons around Sedona, Arizona, in order to find an energy spot that was conductive to writing. He self-published the book. Warner Books bought the rights to the book in 1994 and it became a world-wide bestseller.

The gas station scene illustrates learning to access a different way of being, or as James Redfield writes, "Covert manipulations for energy can't exist if you bring them into consciousness by pointing them out." Most of these hidden manipulations are so habitual that we do not even know we are performing them.

Early in the movie, the main character John arrives at a mountain retreat in Peru and spends some time in the gardens, guided by one of the people who work there, a woman called Sarah. When he sees a beautiful girl sitting on a bench, he walks over and tries to chat with her. The girl, Marjorie, is very sensitive, immediately closes herself off and leaves. John asks his guide what just happened. Sarah smiles and reports what she had observed: that John had been trying to manipulate Marjorie energetically in a typical male conquest way. The film uses CGI effects to show these auric energy flows between the actors. John objects and says he had just been striking up a conversation. He was in his habit mode and as yet unaware of that level of reality. Amorah writes, "What if we simply responded with what our reality was?" As the story unfolds John learns more and more to do just that.

-- *Stephen Muires (editor)*

yell at me?" That will jangle most people out of attack mode, because they have not really thought about it, and it gives them a moment to look at their behavior. If they say they want an answer, and if we can answer from our center, then we answer. If we cannot, we say, "Look, because of the way you approached me, I've gotten defensive right now. I'd like to answer your question, but I'm going to do it a little later when I am more centered." What if we just did not communicate with negative emotion? What if we chose to break the dialogue when we noticed that we were going into a matching frequency with each other on an ego level—to break the dynamic?

This world has taught us that when things go wrong, somebody is doing something to us, and we have to answer them with the same energy they sent to us. In order to be strong enough to repel their negativity, we have to hit back with ours. It is like a fist fight. It is like two bulls going head to head. Even if we justify the defensiveness because we felt attacked, we are still like a bull going head to head, because defensiveness is a violent energy.

Do you know what I mean when I talk about defensiveness? It is when we answer with a charge: we are proving ourselves, but we are doing it by making someone wrong at the same time. It is really a counterattack. We become the very thing we are reacting to, but we righteously justify it because someone else did it first. I think we need to help each other remember that when we are on a spiritual path, every moment of our lives is part of that path. It is more than the ten minutes or the hour that we take to meditate once a day. Being on our spiritual path encompasses more than just the time we are at a workshop, meditation, or satsang.[17] If we are really and truly on a spiritual path, it is our life. That means: every moment we are to live in the right way.

The other thing I would like to say in terms of unity in diversity is that our world is made up of many cultures, each having their own rules. In the past I have worked with people from all over the world and also from different states here in the United States. Even traveling from the state of Mississippi to California is like traveling through several foreign countries. We each come from very unique cultural backgrounds. We assume, because we are brought up to live in a very self-centered world, that we know how it is supposed to be. Sometimes

---

[17] Editor's note: *satsang* is a Sanskrit word which means "sitting in truth." This usually involves listening to or reading Hindu scriptures in the company of other people.

the basic ways of living of other people seem really stupid to us.

I had a realization once. There was this woman who wanted to work with me. She was from a foreign country. She was in a very abusive marriage. Her husband was against the spiritual movement, and she did her spiritual work behind his back. I told her at one point that I did not feel I could do sessions with her, if her lifestyle is supporting the re-creation of her problem. I realized afterward that I really and truly had the thought she would have to divorce her husband unless he was willing to change. However, she also had clearly told me that in her culture people never divorce; they marry for life. I had to stop and realize that my spiritual idea of leaving a place of ego and control was counter to her spiritual idea that marriage is for life, no matter what. I realized that I needed to honor her spiritual reality and not try to convince her that her marriage was holding her back. If I was going to work with this woman, I had to understand her spiritual need as she saw it, not as I saw it.

As healers and teachers in the world, we have a certain intelligence and understanding gained from our own spiritual path, from watching what works for others and what does not, and from reading books. There is a line in the film *Brother Sun, Sister Moon,* where St. Francis talks about the sin of presumption. One of his followers has been killed by the soldiers who want to banish the ways of St. Francis. After discovering this, St. Francis decides to do a pilgrimage to speak to the Pope and find out why this has happened. "Has he failed the people through the sin of presumption?" he asks himself. I think that we sometimes all are a little guilty of the sin of presumption: we assume we know what is better for someone than they know for themselves. I have gone through many layers of this issue over the years as a healer.

I learned a long time ago that I am not in a healing session to make a person see it my way. I am there to facilitate their higher purpose. In order to do that, I even changed the format of my sessions. I used to answer questions, but I do not do that anymore. I tell the person at the beginning of the session that I am going to ask their higher self what is going to help them achieve their purpose in this lifetime, and that will be the focus. My session is based on that rather than on what I clairvoyantly perceive the person's needs to be—because I may be off, or they may not be ready for that healing, or it may not be something they want to change. As a healer who holds a multidimensional space, I have a great ability to impact someone's reality, and I want to be sure that I am telling them something that is totally right.

Brother Sun, Sister Moon

This 1972 film, directed by Franco Zeffirelli, portrays the life of Saint Francis of Assisi (1181-1226). The film is old-fashioned and a little melodramatic.

Francis has visions of Christ and begins to establish a church based on extreme humility. This later became the Franciscan Order. Francis sways many people by his preaching and his visions, which results in the incident that Amorah mentions. A follower gets killed and Francis blames himself. He wonders if knowing something and trying to apply it to others may be wrong, a presumption to think that it is valid for them too.

The climax of the film is when Francis gets an audience with the pope, who then miraculously endorses his humility and his unorthodox approach to God. Francis asks if he has made a mistake presuming to know what God wants him to do. The pope answers: "Errors will be forgiven. In our obsession with original sin, we too often forget original innocence. Don't let that happen to you."
-- *Stephen Muires (editor)*

I really want to impress on you this idea: when we think we know what someone is doing, when we think we know who they are, when we think we know why they are so suspicious, or why we are suspicious of them, when we have ideas that we know what they need to do in order to be okay, then we are living in a very ego deceptive space no matter how 'correct' we might sound.

The biggest thing I see breaking up unity in diversity is relationships. Ironically, this is where we are meant to learn about unity in diversity. If we are in a relationship with someone, especially a sexual relationship or a close friendship, we are meant to learn how to love enough to want the person to have free will. We are meant to love enough to want to give them respect, to care about our impact on them, and not try to change them to meet our perfect picture so our life will finally be okay.

Most people go into relationships with preconceived ideas of what it means to be a loving person. If their partner does not meet those ideas, they think it means that person does not love them. We have many expectations, and expectations are based on who we are, what our history and our cultural upbringing is. What our partner does may be based on a very different cultural upbringing, a different set of goals and a totally different set of expectations that are absolutely right for them. If they are not right for them ultimately, they are right for them now, or else they would not be doing what they are doing. They need to learn from their actions.

No one can ever behave beyond their current level of growth, understanding and evolution. If a person is behaving in a way that you know is not ideal, all that tells you is their growth is relative to a specific issue at the present moment. It does not tell you they are bad or wrong. It just says where they are right now. If a person lies to you, they are not doing that to you. They are just being where they are on their path and doing what they do. That is the only interpretation anything ever needs. However, if you choose to take it personally, you miss the point of truth entirely.

If you are really interested in someone in some way, and that person lies to you, steals from you, or gossips behind your back, and you take it personally, then that is an ego reaction which breaches divine love, divine trust, unity in diversity, and surrender to divine will. In surrender to divine will, you observe, register, and make choices based on love. You do not stop the love. You trust that ultimately each person will get the lessons they need, and ultimately they are perfect. If they cannot share your truth in this moment, then it is your responsibility to be discerning. In this world of relationships, magnetism happens. You want to think that this is the one, or that you are destined to have a short-term sexual relationship, or that this is the best friend you can ever have. The first time that person breaches your ideas, you are furious, because you were counting on them.

Here is the next question: did you ever ask them if they were willing to give what you presumed? Did you ever stop and say: "I need to know that you can promise me you won't talk to other people about the personal intimacies we share, because these are things I'm working on in my life that I don't want other people having judgments about. I want to work on it in an intimate way with you as my friend. Do you agree?" If the person says, "Yes," then there is a certain level of trust. If they go out and gossip about it anyway, then never again share those things which you wanted to keep private. It is that simple. The person wanted to give a level of trust but obviously could not; they are not at that point in their growth yet, so do not share anything important. Do not start out sharing the core secret of your life. Maybe you can test a little, and let things build up in the natural evolution of relationships.

Instead, you tend to have magnetisms based on past lives. "Yes, I remember when we ascended together in Bali." Vroom! You are off and running. All of our trust, love, and sex gets wrapped up in that person within an hour of knowing them. We say, "It must be destined because we've done it before. I know we're meant to be together, because the moment I felt you, all of our chakras aligned and bonded." I am sorry, it is not true. Rather, that is a rampage of new age deceptions. We have all been guilty of it. I have learned it the hard way. I have done it over and over again. I cannot tell you how much I have entered into relationships with naivety and ended up damaged for it, but the only one who ever hurt me was me.

You have to grow up and be a little more responsible for your life. You assume that if someone loves you, they will not act in a certain way. That person may really and truly love you, but they may not yet have outgrown a certain tendency. You need to know that, before you place your trust in them and then blame them.

If you want to live in unity in diversity, then you owe it to every single living human to give them basic human respect. Basic human respect requires never expecting something of someone that they have not told you they will give. Basic human respect requires not handing out advice without asking if the person wants it. If someone is an alcoholic and people are going to intervene, I think that person first has to say, "Yes, I'm willing." If the person says, "No, leave me alone," then leave them alone. You could tell them, "I love you. I care about your life. If there's a point when you do decide you want help, I'll be happy to help you."

People in the new age seem to think that they know where the other person is coming from and that they should tell them about it. They do not stop to ask if the person wants to hear it. They do not stop to ask the person about what was going on for them in that situation. They just tell them what they did. "When we were together yesterday and you said such and such, I felt you were really angry with me and not being willing to be honest about it. I thought we were better friends than that, and I'm really questioning our friendship." That is a typical conversation when a person thinks they are being responsible. I think a responsible conversation would go: "I want to talk to you about something. Is now a good time?" If you get a 'yes,' you keep going. "Do you remember yesterday when we were in this particular situation? I was wondering what you were feeling when you said such and such?" Then you wait to find out. If the person starts to squirm a little or does not remember, then say, "I'd like to tell you what it felt like for me." If you get a go ahead, then say, "It felt to me like you were angry about something, but didn't want to say it. Is that true? And if so I'd really like to know what you're angry about, because I'd like to keep our relationship clean." Then the person may respond and tell you what was going on with them. After they have shared, your next response would be, "Thank you for telling me." Before you try to counter anything they have said, thank them for being honest. Then, if you are not sure how you think or feel about it, suggest you talk again later.

Do not go around reading peoples' lives uninvited; that is very invasive. When you tell a person where they are coming from, often what is going on is that your ideas have resulted from some action or words that reminded you of something in your past, and that created contraction in, say, your third chakra and you felt attacked. Ultimately the whole thing was because they reminded you of when as a child your mother sent anger into your third chakra, when you were trying to be nice. The person may not have had an agenda. If somebody sincerely says to you that they did not feel angry toward you, you have to assume they are telling the truth. Then make it your issue instead of continuing to blame them.

No one can injure you if you are radiating outward and not in reaction to what they are doing. What gets you injured is that you react to the other person not giving you the response you want, and you contract against it. The moment you start contracting against something, you pull it to yourself. When you see that a person is incapable or unwilling to step off attack-defense mode, it becomes your responsibility to stop trying to get them to listen. A person in that mode is only listening from the ego. There is no one home. Do not try to talk to them; they are not there. If you are trying to communicate, you are willing to hear their version and to love them, and they come back at you in an attacking and defensive way, you might try another statement. Tell them you do not want to make them angry, but you want to talk about this in a respectful way. If they respond with an attack, then ask if you can discuss it later. Why would you want to stay and feed a negative ego? All you are doing is supporting their false identity by engaging it and trying to convince them of something else. It will not work.

I would like to give an example from my own life. I was in a relationship and I was trying to find a way to get past the person's defenses. I realized what I was doing and finally said, "When you're ready to talk to me from a place of love and supporting each other in getting through this, then we'll continue. Right now this doesn't serve either of us." Then I said, "Good night," and hung up the phone. I did not slam the phone down accusing him of not being ready to get real. I just spoke my truth and I disengaged, because I was talking to someone's ego that was in survival attack mode. There was no way truth was going to get in.

If you are really wanting to come from truth and not just wanting to make your point, get the person to see you. If you are attached to the need for the person to hear what you have to say, then your hanging in there complicates the problem. The very fact that you are attached to their hearing you draws their energy into you. They are not necessarily standing there putting cords into your body, even if their energy is out there. If your aura is radiating compassion, light and non-judgment with no attachment, negative energy just bounces off. Light that is radiating out has no magnetism, even for a really angry person. If you feel you cannot do it alone, then immediately call for help from your guides. Push the other person ethereally out of your aura. Then seal your aura in a bubble, and ask for help. Do not engage while your light is not radiating. Tell them you cannot talk right now and you will get back to them. Or ask them if they want to hear what you have to say. If they say "no," then do not offer it.

You get very attached when talking to people. You want to be heard. You get very attached to getting them to see that you did not do anything wrong. The very fact that you are attached is like a psychical hook into them: everything that they are feeling comes pouring into you. If you do not want to be attacked, then get out of paranoia and get out of attachment. Those are the real keys.

There are many ways to process your feelings after such an encounter. You can sit down and write anger/hate letters and imagine reading them to the person you encountered. If you are going to do this, then you need to clear your environment. The following is one of the ways to do that.

Clearing the environment

1. Ask St. Germaine to fill and seal the room with violet flame.

2. Ask Archangel Michael to seal the room with the sword of truth and to isolate you in a bubble so you can move the anger and hate that is in your body right now, without psychically harming anyone or drawing harm to yourself.

3. Now act out any behavior you feel a need to express. You can hit them, swear at them, yell and scream, and it is not going to hurt anyone. Have it in the back of your mind the whole time you are acting, that you are going beyond the act to truth.

I think the reason that people in the new age and in general constantly seem to come back to anger and suspicion, is because they clear emotions but they do not clear the attitudes behind the emotions. When you are doing your emotional processing, you can beat on the pillows, cry, and have the most wonderful emotional clearing. A week later, when somebody triggers the same issue, there is just as much to go through, because you have not changed the underlying belief or attitude. You have not changed the thought that created your reactions.

We have got to learn to catch it quicker and quicker, until we get to the point where we prevent it. Then finally we come to the point where it does not even come up, because we have naturally transmuted the tendency and transformed the attitude. This does not mean you are constantly questioning yourself and your thoughts, looking for harmful agendas. Nor do you need to scrutinize yourself and be paranoid about yourself. If a negative thought or negative attitude comes up, notice it, then cancel it, and move on with your day. You do not have to sit and process all the time.

This can turn into a problem: people who are into perceiving the psychic arena get caught up in who is doing what to whom all the time. Their own paranoia gets them caught up in the astral planes, more than what anyone else had ever thought of doing to them could have. When something is going on, deal with it in the moment as simply, clearly, directly, and impeccably as you can. Then move on and forget about it. If you find yourself thinking about it, use the sword of truth.

For example, sometimes I find myself thinking about someone who hurt my feelings two months ago, although I have gone through forgiveness work and resolved it with them. But there is still something lingering which reminds me of the issue, and once again I find myself having a conversation in my mind about it. The moment I am aware I am doing that, I take out my sword of truth and slice through it. I say, "I don't need to give that any more attention." Then I move on with my day. If it keeps coming back over and over again, then I know it is something deeper, and I might set aside time to look at the issue.

But, to summarize, if you can just slice through it, decide that it needs no more of your attention, and move on, that is the best. When you are over-processing and looking into every feeling you have, it gets absurd, because you are here to express divine spirit in a body. Do not forget that. When getting caught up in the healing and clearing and when being suspicious about what is going on all the time, do not forget to stop, go into no-mind, breathe, and be gentle for a while.

If you do not want to use the sword of truth, then use a rainbow flame or a violet flame torch. The moment you are indulging in negative thought or you are rehearsing a conversation with someone you feel defensive toward, take out the torch and repeat: "That needs no more of my attention." Then go on with your day. You might also need to sit and remind yourself, "It's true that I felt hurt by what this person did, but I recognize that it's just them being themselves; it wasn't personal against me. Anyone in that situation would have reacted the same way." You choose to not let it be a problem for you. You choose to love and respect the person for exactly where they are on their path right now. You don't choose to put yourself into situations in which you know they do not have the growth to be accountable. That is being responsible.

Do not go around trying to hold people accountable for something they are not able to be. Do not go around holding people accountable for something they have not said they would give. That would be waiting to prove this person wrong so you can say, "See, I should have known better." The world is not doing anything to you that your own thoughts have not created. If you say that you are not creating this thing someone does to you over and over again, then ask yourself: "Why is something happening over and over again? Why am I putting myself in a position for it to happen again?" Take some responsibility and stop placing yourself in the same situations with the same agendas.

Every thought, every energy, and every attitude has a frequency. That frequency seeks out corresponding frequencies and aligns you with something. For example, if you want to have a sacred marriage, you have to be sending out energy of sacred marriage, not an energy of "there's no man or woman out there who's ever going to be loving enough. What's wrong with these people anyway?" If that is the frequency you are dwelling on, then it does not matter how much you justify it with your life experiences. That is what will be drawn back to you. Rise above the past, instead of allowing it to rule your thoughts and your reactions. If you have a contracted reaction to something, it is always your issue.

It is time for us to learn how to live life in an innocent and childlike way. A child watches what happens in life with awe and wonder. A child has a lot of curiosity and thinks it is really fun when someone else does something totally different from what they would do. They might think, "Wow! That person does a lot of things differently than I do. I wonder why?" They then go and ask.

Children do not judge differences so quickly. They observe and learn from them. In order to live in true unity in diversity, in Oneness with everyone and everything, we must learn to approach life in this manner, to see the amount of variety there is in existence, and to celebrate it. We can learn to love everything and everyone at all times no matter what is happening. Then we will be on our path to unity in diversity.

13 Love and Oneness

Love is the opening door to Oneness with All That Is.

Once you have learned to love every part of yourself...once you have learned to love everything and everyone from your past...once you have found your multidimensional alignment...once you have fully found equality between male and female...once you have learned to love and not control people...once you have found invincibility of spirit...and once you have learned to live in unity in diversity...you have arrived!

Oneness happens when you have learned to experience unconditional love in both the giving and the receiving. You become the vehicle for it. You are it. This Oneness comes from being able to look at everything and everyone, embodied and in multiple dimensions, and to instantly melt into them the same way the Holy Mother and Holy Father did initially. This cycle of melting into Oneness

> Oneness happens when you have learned to experience unconditional love.

with each other and then individuating again, then melting into Oneness and repeating the cycle, is the main key to movement within all existence.

The movement of the orbits of planets, stars and whole galaxies is based on this cycle. You have those movements within your body. Every cell has an orbital pattern. Every organ and gland has a co-created orbital pattern. Your thoughts and empty mind have this eternal cycle of movement at their source. Your entire body self has a unique relationship to the whole.

You are like a single cell in the body of existence. Yet the health of each cell is vital to the overall health of the whole. If one single cell in your body becomes diseased, it starts a chain reaction into other cells and eventually becomes a disease or malfunction of the body. Maybe you start to walk stiffly and sit hunched over. Maybe you become rigid in your thinking. Maybe you get cancer.

The whole is moving to a place and time when all of the cells in the body of Oneness are healthy and are helping to create a healthy whole. Your attitudes and beliefs are what create that. Yes, you! Each and every one of you.

What you think, you create. If you truly believe in being poor, you will be poor. If you truly believe in abundance, you will have abundance. If you believe you have a lot of clearing and processing to do, that will be your reality. If you really believe you are already there and live it in your heart and mind, then you are already there. There is no exception to this rule.

St. Germaine told me years ago that we are allowed to create what we really want. Then he told me to always specifically ask that the things we want are created within the harmonics of co-creation. This simply means that what is created will be the right thing for everything and everyone in existence. It will be a win-win for All That Is. It does not imply that when we are creating we must hold back a little, just in case it is not in alignment with All That Is. We are simply asked to hold the intention that it will be a win-win reality for everyone and everything.

It will be amazing when everyone creates their reality from this space. Amazing outcomes will come about by living in unity in diversity with a genuine desire for a win-win reality—in harmony with All That Is. We want health and happiness for all, no matter what their place in existence is.

When we have arrived at that sacred place within ourselves, the final realization of Oneness will come from the deep knowing that everything and everyone is an equal part of that wholeness and that we are all connected to one another. We are not just like a cell within the whole. We are all a part of that whole, and infinitely connected. What we do and think affects all of existence.

If we hold judgment or negativity, it affects All That Is in a chain reaction. Healthy actions affect All That Is in the same way. Holding limited beliefs in any capacity creates a limitation in the reality of others. Holding blame, resentment, belief in betrayal, lack of forgiveness, means that we literally contribute to the continuation of war. Changing these issues becomes imperative for each and every one of us.

When those changes have become fully actualized within us, Oneness is. You can experience that Oneness whether others have completed their learning, growing and changing or not. Within existence there is a part within each personality that still exists on an original creation level. Your soul essence is eternal. When you have healed all of the issues we spoke of earlier, what you have actually done is reclaim the true self that has always existed. You simply gave away your identity to your limited ego. When you have fully reclaimed your true self, you step into an existence in which everything and everyone already exists at that level of essence.

Is it not amazing that this reality is with you at all times, and you simply have not yet come into awareness of it? Are you ready now? Are you willing to be the best that you can be? Are you able to see the best in everything and everyone? You must see that in that reality the earth already is at peace. The liar is truthful. The killer is harmless. All that we have judged or held prejudice about is already non-existent. Your attitudes, thoughts, and beliefs can show you a new reality now. It is up to you, and only you.

You are the master of your universe—only you. What you do and how you live is your choice and yours alone. When individual beings within existence moved into having issues that needed to be healed and a true identity that needed to be reclaimed, the universal laws were brought into being. Universal law says that you have free will. You can make choices about everything. The guides will not interfere with free will. You are not allowed to interfere with anyone else's free will. Therefore, you are the master and chooser of the reality you live in. This is another eternal truth.

Giving power over to others such as a guru, teacher, life partner, president, or friend is a free will choice you make. It will alter your experiences, but only because you chose for it to do so. It is time now to un-choose giving your power away. It is time now to re-become the conscious creator of your destiny. You are the One. You are the master. It is 100% up to you, and no one else.

The key to being this master creator of your own reality is love. Behind every decision, every thought, every feeling, love is the opening door. Love is the most healing and unifying energy within existence—infinitely and eternally. Fully giving and receiving love is ultimately the way of your essence. It is who you are. It is the divine nature of all of existence. Let us move into this wholeness of love now, by going through a meditation to complete this return to

Oneness.

Ending meditation
---

1. Call upon your higher self to be with you for this meditation time. Tell him/her that you know that you are the master of your life and that you have universal free will.

2. Call upon all of the guides of light: ascended masters, personal guides, angels and archangels of light, Pleiadian and Sirian emissaries of light, the Holy Mother and Holy Father of All That Is. Ask them to join you.

3. Ask all of these beings of light to surround you and fill you with their love, as much as you are capable of receiving. Lie down and receive this love from them as deeply as you can, for as long as you want.

4. Give them your love in return as much as is possible.

5. Ask all of these beings of light to blend with you into Oneness, as much as is possible at this time. Relax and blend.

6. Call upon the higher-dimensional connection to the essence of everyone in existence. Also call upon the higher-dimensional connection to the essence of every planet and star in existence. Blend with them fully, or as much as you can at this time, for as long as you wish.

7. When you are ready to move on, tell all of the light beings and essence beings that you are One with them now and always. Tell them you only want whatever is to the highest good for all of them and yourself, a win-win for everyone and everything.

8. Relax and feel yourself aligning with them in the harmonics of co-creation, and realize that they all want the same reality as you.

9. Ask your higher self to assist you in maintaining this ongoing connection to Oneness with All That Is.

10. Take a few deep breaths and bring yourself back to your day.

Know that you can do this meditation as often as you wish. It will continue to go deeper and deeper each time. And remember you are the only master of your fate. Oneness with the divine All That Is and with all of yourself is your divine destiny. You are that.

ABOUT THE AUTHOR

Amorah Quan Yin was born in Irvine, a small town in Kentucky, on November 30, 1950. She passed away on June 13, 2013, after an auto accident on Everett Memorial Highway, Mt. Shasta, California.

Amorah was a natural healer and psychic since birth. She adopted the name Amorah Quan Yin in 1993 after a direct experience of Quan Yin during meditation. She lived in Mt. Shasta for 24 years and there founded the Dolphin Star Temple in 1998. She often said that Mt. Shasta was the only place she ever felt at home. She loved the mountain for its high and unique energy and for the beauty of the surrounding nature.

Amorah wrote 4 books before *Oneness*. *The Pleiadian Workbook*, *The Pleiadian Tantric Workbook*, *Pleiadian Perspectives on Human Evolution*, and *Affinity*. These were published in 12 languages. She also recorded hundreds of CDs.

She never wanted to be the center of attention, she was rather shy.

Appendix 1: Interview with Eileen Kelly

Amorah and Me

(Extracted from an interview conducted by Gary Kendall and Ulla Anderen, Mt. Shasta, 2014. In the following pages Eileen Kelly presents personal stories and details of her many years of friendship with Amorah.)

First meeting

I met Amorah at a 4th of July 'Psychic Faire' in 1989 where she was doing readings. I had just lost my beloved and was in a grieving mode. I sat down in front her and she said, "Aha! We need to talk." And she gave me a wonderful healing on the spot. Afterwards, she mentioned that she was offering classes here in Mt Shasta. I signed up and completed the whole FSP (Full Sensory Perception) series, which at that time took a year. It was just one class one weekend a month for a whole year. That first class was very friendly and easy-going. There were five of us, and we met at Amorah's home. We did readings on each other. It was a good thing that it was a safe space, because a lot of deep personal things came up for healing.

My first PLI (Pleiadian Lightwork Intensive) class in 1998 had 29 students. Some of us had blocks that took a long time to clear. As the Pleiadians worked with us through Amorah, the system expanded exponentially and healings happened much faster. By 2004 when she asked me to help during a class, it was just a matter of putting our fingers on the points and 'zap'—the Ka flowed through.

Around this time, Amorah and I spent a lot of time out in nature and with her singing, which was Amorah's greatest joy in life. This evolved into her receiving much of the original music she later recorded on her music CD's.

The early travels

In 1996 Amorah had written the first book and was looking for the appropriate publisher. Through guidance she sent it to Bear & Company, which was owned by Barbara Hand Clow's husband. When Barbara read the manuscript, she knew it was the 'how to' for the book she had just completed on the Pleiadians. She and Amorah almost immediately put together a world tour including England, Scotland, Egypt, Greece, and Bali in order to share the work and to promote their books. Amorah continued to do annual tours to 'power spots' around the world, which resulted in many groups of students coming to Mt Shasta (her favorite power spot) to attend the Mystery School.

Amorah in Delphi, Greece (1997).

Keiko Anaguchi of Tokyo read Amorah's book, *Pleiadian Workbook, Awakening the Divine Ka,* and fell in love with the teachings and Amorah. A deep friendship developed as Keiko came to Mt Shasta for extended periods of time to receive the training. Later she started bringing groups of Japanese students with her to experience Amorah personally. The first time Amorah went to Japan was with OmaKayuel (Peter Reese), her husband at the time. In Japan they stayed at Keiko's home. Amorah was not feeling well and ended up contracting SARS. Fortunately, she was able to get out of Japan and go to Australia, OmaKayual's home, for healing. But it was touch and go for a while.

After that, she was reluctant to go to Japan for quite some time. But as her health improved and her relationship with Keiko deepened, she responded to Keiko's desire to share this work with more people in Japan and went there several times. Her support of Keiko's desire to spread the teachings evolved into the development of the Dolphin Star Temple Japan. I was on the Board of Directors of Dolphin Star Temple during that time. A core group and I here in Mt Shasta were surprised to see the development of a different teaching structure, but Amorah always did what felt right to her.

The golden years

Some of the best days for me with Amorah were in the beginning when she would just show up at my door. I was still going through deep grieving from the loss of the love of my life. One afternoon I opened the door and there stood Amorah who immediately asked, "Something I can do for you?" She came in and started running energy for several hours while sitting on my bed. Such a blessing she was! She just felt what I needed and showed up for me.

During the PLI classes, she would do a 'check-in' every morning, even with all 29 people going through their stuff. It started at ten o'clock in the morning, and by two o'clock we were still doing check-in. During that time the students were experiencing huge shifts in their lives and were reconsidering their life priorities. Often, it was discovered that money and success and all that superficial stuff just didn't cut it. As I understand 'check in,' it is still used as the opening of each day's class, though, I am sure, it moves much faster these days, as does all the work.

Amorah originally expanded the FSP system after working with a teacher who was trained at the Berkeley Psychic Institute. Following that, she began receiving information from the Pleiadians about the opening of the Ka body, which evolved into the Pleiadian Lightwork Intensive (PLI) classes and the Dolphin Moves. FSP, PLI and Dolphin Moves became the basis for the *Dolphin Star Temple Mystery School of Pleiadian Lightwork* around 1995. Shortly after that, she petitioned the state of California for non-profit status officially establishing The Dolphin Star Temple as a church.

The Ka system was channeled, as was most of the PLI work. Amorah was at a hot spring somewhere, sitting in the water, when it started coming to her. We spent a lot of time out in nature, because it was conducive to releasing blocks to the flow of information. One time we went up to Gumboot Lake and there were these tiny brand new flowers in clusters. They were pulling us to them. We stood over them, and it was like having an orgasm. They were *that* alive. Both of us went into a bliss place for hours. These were Amorah's golden years.

Amorah regularly did phone readings right from the beginning. She had a constant flow of requests. When she started going to Japan, she had calls from groups of people from there as well.

Amorah's early life

Amorah was the oldest of five children. Her birthfather (not her stepfather) was apparently not completely sane. Amorah recounted memories of him trying to suffocate her as a baby in her crib. She had physical memory of this. She was very close with her grandmother. Granny Benton taught her how to bake making everything from scratch, which

Amorah at Gumboot Lake. (Picture by Eileen.)

throughout her life Amorah loved to do and share.

Amorah's stepfather was a very strict fundamental Baptist preacher. She would listen to his sermons and hear the message: "Love everyone, everybody is equal"—stuff like that. But when she had several black friends in college, including a black boyfriend, her parents found it completely unacceptable, which ultimately caused a lifelong break in their relationship.

At one point during her collage years, she became extremely ill and went home to heal. For many months she investigated holistic healing methods and eventually discovered that she was environmentally allergic, which she dealt with for a large part of her life.

In the period right after college, Amorah had a job as the housemother for a group of mentally handicapped kids. She shared with me about her experiences with them and how being with these young people opened up her heart.

In the 80's Amorah spent time with Osho (Bhagwan Shree Rajneesh) at Rajneeshpuram in Oregon. This was before she lived in the San Francisco Bay area where she took classes and did psychic healing, and before she came to Mt. Shasta. She knew quite a few people from that community, and many came to visit her here in Mt Shasta. As far as I know, she left before the breakdown of the Osho community in 1985.

In one of the very first FSP classes, Osho showed up in the room. He had made his transition, though we didn't know that at the time. Amorah recognized him right away, but she had a policy that no one's guru could be in the training room, and she told him, "This is not appropriate; you need to get out of here." He left, but it was an interesting experience for us. This started her talking about gurus and what she perceived as their way of taking over a person's free will. She didn't have a lot of patience for them after her experiences in the past. It seemed to her like Osho had been trying to influence her, pushing her to do something that she didn't want to do. She warned her students that with gurus it was easy to become a slave.

Fame

Amorah herself was aware that her unusual capabilities meant she needed to give up certain things, that being famous was not all it's cracked up to be. In the early years there were quite a few pangs of jealousy within the spiritual community of Mt Shasta about Amorah's rise to fame. She was one of the first to have a successful book and to have students coming from all over the world to study with her. I had a personal experience with a woman who was renting rooms to Amorah's students, and at the same time telling people that Amorah's work was not Christ-centered. I had a big reaction to this, but when I told Amorah, she had no reaction and just said "People have a right to their own opinion."

She did have to learn to set some boundaries. She loved to go for drives with people, but often they'd be asking the whole time, "Do you see this? And what about that?" I think that one of the reasons she liked to hang around with me was because I didn't do that with her. Having been psychic since childhood, I had learned about boundaries for myself. Amorah and I could just be quiet together without invading each other's space. I am sure that is one of the reasons we were friends for such a long time. I was someone who didn't elevate her or put her up on a pedestal. She appreciated that I didn't expect her to be high and mighty and not have a real life.

The teacher-student dynamic

Amorah loved training practitioners and teachers, she felt she had found her purpose. She wrote a Code of Ethics for practitioners to follow and was always updating the class materials.

Many of the teachers were getting new students and clients through the DST website. Amorah's attitude was the students that are yours will come to you. We were all on a practitioners list on the web site, and people would look at the list and see who lit up for them. If someone went from one teacher or practitioner to another, there were no hard feelings and no sense of competition. That was key in her original teaching. I know for myself that sometimes things came up that I was uncomfortable handling, so I'd send the client on to someone else. Amorah herself sent people on to other practitioners as well.

Crystals and the stores

Sometime in the early 2000's , Amorah met a man named Tony Raw at a Wesak festival in Mt Shasta, and he handed her a crystal from Namibia, Africa. As soon as he placed the crystal in her hand, she went into a past life experience where she remembered information about the healing properties of these crystals and received a lot of specific information about them. Amorah was so inspired about the specialness of the Namibian Crystals that she decided to make them available to her students, even though she thought she was complete using crystals. She often said these "beings" were very special and held energies specific to humanity 's needs for this particular time on the planet.

Amorah set up a room for the crystals in her home and I was there when we received the first box. It was a huge box and had to be delivered by the freight company in a big truck. I opened up the box, and immediately I could feel these

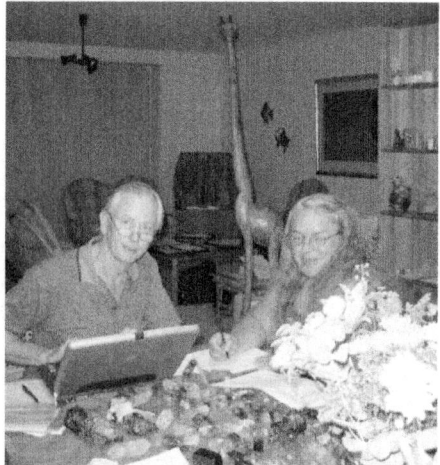

Tony & Amorah with the Namibian crystals

crystals connecting with the mountain. The energy was just going back and forth, they were talking to each other. It was absolutely palpable.

The opening of her first store in 2004 was another breaking-out endeavor for Amorah and provided an outlet for something she loved to do, which was buying lots of beautiful things. She provided a space for local artists to show their work and offered space for travelling teachers to do classes. She also had regular meditation and channeling evenings in the store, which she continued to do until the end.

Amorah's last store was the realization of her dream of having a presence on the main street in downtown Mt Shasta. In addition to offering a large display of Namibian Crystals, it included local artwork, jewelry and lots of Dolphin items, a display of the one hundred twenty channeled CD's, her six music CD's, three DVD's, and her four books in twelve languages. It offered her complete body of work to the public.

Relationships

The one thing Amorah felt she missed in this life was a long lasting intimate relationship. She had no children, and she filled this void by becoming a Godmother to several children. One who was with her until the end had been a neighbor. Whisper tells the story of coming to visit Amorah, knocking on the door, with her little brother in tow. When Amorah answered, Whisper's mouth opened in awe. She cried out, "You are an angel," and, of course, the children were invited in for cookies and milk, and they kept coming back. Soon after that, this beautiful little girl asked Amorah to be her Godmother, and theirs became a relationship Amorah treasured for the rest of her life.

One of the things Amorah said to me more than once was that our relationship was the longest she had with anyone who wasn't family.

Amorah's health and her driving

One of Amorah's greatest challenges in this life was her body and body image. She was always a big woman continuing a heritage from her father's family. Amorah sustained an injury to her leg on a trip to Greece in the 90's that bothered her for the rest of her life. Later on, she was also diagnosed with diabetes and had high blood pressure, for which she was taking medication. In the early 2000's her high blood pressure had caused her to become blind in one eye.

Amorah loved to drive fast and once told me, "I feel like I just have to slam the peddle to the metal." When I would say something about her fast driving, she would laugh at me. I told her, "I'm not afraid of dying. I'm afraid of getting hurt." Ultimately her driving became a major issue in our relationship. About four years before her fatal accident when I was meditating, Archangel Michael said to me, "You are not to get in Amorah's car again." When I told Amorah that I could not ignore my guidance and would not be riding with her anymore, it created our only major breakdown in communication.

When I was notified that she had been in a serious accident on Mt Shasta, I was not surprised to hear she had gone around a curve too fast and lost control. She was so badly injured that Mt. Shasta hospital had to airlift her to a larger hospital. She died 10 days later. Her youngest sister Anglia, who was visiting from Kentucky, was in the car with Amorah and sustained a broken arm and back injury. I understand she has recovered after having surgery.

The last years

Amorah was always a generous person and a very loving friend. She had on-and-off been somewhat depressed, but more so in her last years. She had always been able to bring herself out of it. With her health problems accumulating and the classes getting smaller, she talked about retiring for a long time. She wasn't at the point where she was willing to downsize and give up some of her lifestyle. But for at least 10 years she was talking about retiring.

Even though she had trained hundreds of practitioners and had as many clients for readings and healings as she wanted, the Dolphin Star Temple organization was not expanding. But Amorah's teaching was that each person should develop his or her own business. She said, "I give you this, and you take it into the world, and you'll do what you'll do with it." This is what really attracted me to becoming part of the organization initially. It wasn't the guru deal. This was very important to me as a person. She was thankful that people moved on and did well. It wasn't a strict teaching like the church. But there was desire for there to be a central support system from DST, and Amorah did have 'Practitioner Days' where she was available to speak to students and teachers.

Amorah received many appreciation letters, saying things like, "You've changed my life." Toward the end, she got to a point where she couldn't receive the acknowledgements anymore. I'm not exactly sure why.

So many people were impacted by her life, her presence, and her teachings. After her death, hundreds of condolence communications filled with the stories of loving appreciation for this outstanding human being were received. Personally, I am blessed to feel that our relationship is complete and am grateful for the dynamic memories.

Appendix 2:

Comments

From

Former

Students

Shared by Mira-El

Amorah moved to Mt. Shasta around 1986 from somewhere near the bay area. She had a jewelry business at that time, and she also baked sweets for Mountain Song, the largest health food store at the time.

She had studied with someone who studied at the Berkeley Psychic Institute, which is where a lot of the basic self-care tools came from. At the very beginning of her teaching, Amorah evolved from doing sessions for people to teaching them to do it for themselves. The 'clairvoyant training program' developed naturally from these beginnings. This was the foundation for the FSP trainings. Also at this time, Amorah was contacted by the Pleiadians, and then the Ka activations and the rest of the PLI material came into the field. I took the clairvoyant training program starting in April 1995, and completed all the trainings and apprenticeships in the next four years.

My most enjoyable times were playing guitar and singing with Amorah and during PLI's, while the students were working with Ka activations and other hands-on sessions. Supporting the emotional well-being of everyone through the beauty and love of music was my greatest joy. I also felt the joy as a teacher of seeing the 'lights go on' in the students as they 'got' what was being presented in class, and experiencing my teacher-self becoming obsolete as the students became capable readers and healers.

I especially loved the DBR (Dolphin Brain Repatterning) work as I experienced such deep relaxation in my core from receiving hands on sessions. I was often the 'model' on the table as my body was easy for finding the points and anatomical areas. And I loved getting touched, even by those just learning.

The sense of family was strong in class, as Amorah really loved teaching and welcomed everyone as a divine being. The classes were very juicy and alive. Amorah and I worked well together and complemented each other, as I was 'spare' and she was 'full-bodied' in our styles and approaches. I also really enjoyed teaching the Japanese students here in Mt. Shasta and in Japan, as I have a strong affinity to Japan and its culture. Some of my best times were in class with them.

ONENESS

Shared by Stephanie Rainbow Lightning Elk Wadell, M.A.

'The Big Boss: Amorah Quan Yin, aka Barbara Gentle Deer'

When I met Amorah in person, I was surprised by her size and weight. Her voice and songs sounded like an angel. I expected to see a waif-like, ethereal, tall, highly energetic person. Amorah was exactly the opposite. But whatever her size and weight, she always had command of her teaching environment, whether it was a small or a large group.

I distinctly remember the FSP training in 1999 at her home in Mt. Shasta. We were a small group, only 4 of us, all women. One of the participants entered the foyer for the beginning of the workshop, and Amorah immediately smelled a lingering scent. We had been told no fragrances were allowed on our person or clothes. Amorah demanded that she take everything off or leave. The participant dropped all of her clothes to the floor while the rest of us stood there hoping we were scent free! "But I thought you said no perfumes or scented soap, and I didn't use anything like that," the participant protested. Amorah thought for a split second and said, "Okay, then it was one of those dryer scented sheets you used!" "Yes, you are right," the participant exclaimed. Amorah left us and returned shortly with a clean set of garments.

I learned about many of Amorah's vulnerabilities as a human being on this planet and was amazed that she could not heal herself of these issues. As time passed, Amorah was able to tolerate essential oils, but spoke often of her fatigue from flying, having to smell everyone in the plane. It was almost crippling for her. Through her intimate sharing of her traumas, allergies, struggles with men, weight problems, and other health concerns, I was challenged to open my mind to her teachings and not to her personality or appearance.

Amorah kept a strong boundary with me. She was the expert, the teacher, and the big boss. I was always her student, even after I graduated.

Amorah amazed me with her ability to produce CDs, books, workshops around the world, offering private sessions, graduating more and more lightworkers, priests, priestesses, and managing her non-profit Dolphin Star Temple and gift store, while struggling and sometimes suffering with her own physical limitations, pain, and emotional grief issues. She commanded her life and probably chose her own death's timing.

ONENESS

Shared by Rondah Hornstra

On Amorah's first visit to Australia, she and OmaKayuel stayed for a while just outside the small town where I lived. The cottage was in the bush, and she adored seeing the kangaroos bouncing around in the wild. We went out to lunch in the town, and when her meal came, she asked the waiter where her salad was. He replied that it was on her plate. She replied, "This is not a salad, this is garnish." He replied that she could order a side salad to go with the meal, and she said, "I will not pay extra for a salad that normally is served with the meal."

Amorah was well known for her love of good food by all those who knew her. And we loved her honesty and forthrightness.

Shared by Mika

There are countless things I've learned from the Dolphin Star Temple (DST) and Amorah's teachings. However, one of the most important elements for me currently is love, and how it represents the most ideal way of being.

Growing up, I was very concerned with what everyone thought. It was as if I had big antennas on top of my head, making me hyper-aware of the current situation and whatever needed to be done. I was living according to the values of my parents and the other people around me, which left me feeling like a lifeless robot, my parents' pet. Eventually it felt as though the only thing I was doing on my own accord was breathing.

I attended a few psychological seminars because I wanted to understand why I felt the way I did. The seminars did give me some self-awareness. However, they didn't provide me with the knowledge I needed to reclaim the lost parts of myself and my waning life force. I felt very lost, and this eventually contributed to a serious illness.

At long last, I met Amorah and the teachings of the DST, and my life changed drastically as a result! During the process of deepening my DST studies, I came to realize that as long as I continued to live the way I had up until that point, I wouldn't even be able to maintain the physical processes required for staying alive, let alone grasp the meaning of being my true self.

Amorah always taught with love, and told me that in order to begin living my true purpose, I'd have to decide to start living my life on purpose. She said that rather than fighting myself and denying myself, I should do what I could, and give myself the recognition I deserve. I am still here today because of Amorah and the DST. I am sincerely grateful for all that I was able to receive from her generous spirit.

Shared by Seiko

It has been 13 years since I first picked up Amorah's workbook *Awakening the Divine Ka*. At the time I wasn't even aware of the word spiritual, and I was just giving the exercises in the workbook a try just out of curiosity. But the book eventually connected me with Amorah and initiated a profound change in my life.

While deepening my learning with the DST, I was able to release various beliefs. Prior to this time, the only way I knew how to move forward in my life was through anger. I had developed a victim mentality, and lived my life playing the role of victim every single day. The coward in me had a very difficult time letting go of anger, and there were numerous times when I began to hate myself. But because of Amorah's teachings, I was able to overcome all of my family issues, to love myself fully, and to accept the differences among my family members.

Amorah had a special connection with Japan and was helping Japanese people to awaken. She sang spontaneous, beautiful songs during class. She was mischievous, sweet, strict and charming. It's as if I can still hear her voice and her laughter . . ..

Shared by Yasu

Before the Dolphin Star Temple (DST), I had great difficulty liking people, including myself. I shut out the world around me, and lived my life thinking that I wasn't worthy of being alive. I used to think about ways to end my life that wouldn't burden anyone. But somewhere deep within myself, I had this nagging feeling that I'd regret it if my life ended at that point. I began to feel a desire to enjoy life. I wanted to be happy, and I wanted to meet like-minded people who would accept me as I was. As spirit would have it, I was being led to the DST when I embraced this new-found feeling.

I found the teachings of the DST to be very refreshing. They taught me to communicate honestly with myself first, and then with others. I learned to focus not on my past or future self, but to respect the feelings of the person I am at this moment. I learned that I am not alone, since I have my higher self and beings of light with me at all times. And lastly, I learned that love is truth.

I'd like to express my heartfelt gratitude to Amorah for bringing the teachings forward for this generation.

Shared by Yvonne Soderberg

'My Picture of Amorah'

It is a Sunday in July and I am slowly walking down Mount Shasta Boulevard through the center of Mount Shasta City, experiencing the energies, and just enjoying being there. It is hot, sunny and quiet with few people around.

A very nice orange Mitsubishi Eclipse convertible with the top down comes roaring up a little too fast for what is typical in this quiet town. Amorah is on the go—dressed in turquoise blue with her long blond hair fluttering in the wind. Beautiful Amorah—independent, strong, and talented—a true, extremely committed, self-made person.

Over some years I was participating the PLI courses, and as there were only two of us in the PLI 2 and 3, I had the chance to get pretty close to Amorah. Initially I had the idea that with just two of us, sessions would go faster than usual and that we might be able to finish a bit earlier each day, but no way. Amorah was too committed for that. She was really rigorous with us. It wasn't always easy being so exposed in a learning situation led by the person who had created everything we did, but looking back it was a blessing. As the course was in her home, we shared all our time during the day as well as dinner every now and then. I have some memories I would like to share.

One day I was standing looking out the window when Amorah came up and asked me what I was thinking. "I am worrying about a friend," I said.

"Yvonne, you must never ever worry. It is one of the worst things you can do. See your friend as a powerful person perfectly capable of handling the issues in her life. Worrying is to take the power away from people."

At first I got a little annoyed. I thought I had the right to worry, if I wanted to. And by the way, worrying is a good thing: it shows I care. But after having thought about it, I realized that Amorah was right, of course. I must always view my friend as capable and able to solve the issues in her life. I must support her with that energy instead of diminishing her, telling her what to do, letting her know unconsciously that I don't trust in her ability. I had never thought about the 'concept of worrying' before, and I spend some time pondering the subject while walking the beautiful surroundings of Mt. Shasta. There was a lot to find out, and it gave me some new ways of being in my life.

Amorah and I shared an interest in jewelry. She had quite a lot and used to wear different jewelry every day, knowing I would comment on it. One day she had a wristband with beautiful Moldavites. The guides asked her to put them over my third eye during a meditation and then to wear them for the day It would help opening up a stronger communication with higher dimensions, they communicated. They also advised me to buy a Moldavite and carry it every day.

Amorah gave me all the catalogues and brochures with jewels she could find, so that I should be able to find exactly the right piece. She was so eager to be of service, and she put all her effort into making sure I would get the best. She ordered one from some place on the east coast and had it delivered to her home—without her charging anything. The Moldavite was gorgeous. It was very soothing being in this so very loving and caring energy of hers.

Having finished PLI 3 there was just one more course left in Mt. Shasta for me to attend, and I had already made a decision to participate when I heard that Amorah had been in a car accident. It was so painful to get that message, and somewhere inside of me a memory of her loneliness showed up.

Subsequently I had two meetings with Amorah when I was meditating. In one she was dressed in a wide turquoise blue robe dancing around in joyful happiness in a meadow, and it was then that I realized she was not coming back. When I got the message she had passed on, I was not surprised.

Another person took on the leadership of the course in Mt. Shasta, and I decided to participate, not only for the course, but to come to a completion with Amorah and the fact that she had died. The course was held in Amorah's house. It was kind of weird being among all her beautiful things in her house when she was not there. Even though her spirit was present, it was somehow an issue.

One day I was standing in the kitchen looking at the mountain, dreaming, and I felt someone touching my back. I turned around thinking that it was a participant, but it wasn't. It was Amorah standing there in her physical body. I jumped high in the air and my heart was beating at 200 bps. I had never met a dead person in her physical body before. She was talking to me. She was talking about my future, and I don't remember everything though I was so moved and I was covered in such a wonderful love. It was a great experience that I will always carry with me.

Thank you Amorah for what you have been giving to me and to the world. I am so much looking forward reading your new book.

Shared by Gary Kendall

'Did I Ever Really Know Amorah?'

When I first traveled to Mt. Shasta to study with Amorah, I excitedly anticipated what it would be like to experience her in person. I really had no idea. I had already spent years studying with Peruvian shamans, and they were all quite different from one another. By the time of my first meeting, I had eagerly read my way through Amorah's two workbooks, and I was deeply devoted to doing the exercises. These were the foundation of my daily spiritual practice, and I was ready to go deeper into this work with Amorah as my guide. But it was a shock when I discovered that there was so much more to learn with her and so many more challenges than what the workbooks contained. How could this be? The horizon stretched beyond my imagination! Attending the FSPs and the PLIs for me was like turning a kid loose in a candy store. I had found the place I so longed to be.

And in one class after another I came to know Amorah. I discovered that the same intelligence and clarity that I had experienced in the books was manifested in her classes. So clear, so direct, so loving. And I came to appreciate her capacity to 'see' when teaching the classes—like the day when I had just started PLI1 and I was learning to open Ka channels. I was on the opposite side of the room from Amorah with my back turned to her, and I was working really, really hard. "Gary, are you sure that you are running the energy in the right direction?" she called to me from across the room. She was so right. I discovered that you learn really fast when you are in the room with a teacher who can actually see and confirm everything you are doing.

And she would not settle for us to simply walk through the exercises. I remember the time that Amorah called out two participants in our class, both of whom were going through the motions of the work, but neither of whom were doing their best. They had developed a dislike for each another, and they had allowed this to affect their work. Amorah pulled them out of the class and gave them a good talking to. Neither wanted to lose face and admit it, and no matter how subtle it might have seemed to others, Amorah wouldn't tolerate it. And I remember a time too when she also called me out when I stopped attending to what my 'client' partner was saying to me. "You know you have a habit of tuning out when you think that you have heard it before." That gave me my first glimpse of a pattern that I had exhibited for years, and it took me a long time to totally leave that behavior behind.

Then too, Amorah repeatedly asked me why I bothered focusing so hard on such small details of the work. I wouldn't just 'do it,' I would study it and analyze it. "You are working like an academic." Indeed, I was, and Amorah just left me to find a less stressful way of working on my own. And I rather saw Amorah through an academic's eyes. (I was still a professor back then.) She was so clear and expansive. She had a fantastic intellect. I imagined that I could have deep and intense discussions about new topics with her out of class. But that is when things broke down. Amorah wasn't interested in that kind of conversation; she did not want to conceptualize and systematize. She was interested in being together, in enjoying the time we shared, and I clearly missed something early on that I yearned for when trying to connect with her.

That is not to say that there weren't fabulous times just being together. I remember one dinner when my wife Ulla and I were together with Omakayuel and Amorah at one of her favorite restaurants. We had somehow drifted over to talking about visions of the future. And Amorah said, "I hope that you are not embarrassed talking about sex, are you?" "No, of course," we replied with no idea of what came next. And she then proceeded to talk about a vision that had come to her during intercourse. It was a graphic connection between the tantric energies of sex and the clairvoyance of a visionary. It didn't take long before all other conversation in the restaurant had come to a dead halt, leaving only the sound of Amorah voice describing her experience without a trace of hesitation.

I did think then that I had come to know Amorah as best I could. I knew her as the brilliant psychic, a mind and a heart of immense capabilities. We clearly liked each other even though I began to think that she saw me as some kind of strange bird. I once tried playing some of my *avant garde* computer music for her, music that I myself thought reflected my spiritual life and experience of being a healer. Her response was "I can only think that you are from some really different part of the universe than I am."

When working for this book and gathering together recollections from many people, I came to a different place in my understanding of knowing Amorah. I realized how my personal understanding of Amorah was so much like that of so many other students—we didn't really know her. We all had in some way projected aspects of ourselves onto her. So many people had needed her to be some particular thing for them, to be perfect in some particular way. She wasn't. She couldn't. Many people had experienced a difficult moment when she had fallen off of the pedestal. How could she have said this? How could she have done that? How could it be that she was such a master teacher and yet fail herself in so many aspects of her life? How challenging it was to know this imperfect Amorah! It seems that there was a public persona, held up by each of us in our own way, and a private reality that for many of us created an indecipherable combination. Rather like a rock star, like the Beatles, what the individual represented was so powerful that it obscured their personal limitations. Amorah was the rock star of our personal spiritual evolutions.

And yet, of course, all of these sides of Amorah came together in her person, especially for me, in the ways that she was uncompromising. I think that the single most important inspiration that I received from Amorah was about the absolute sovereignty of the individual: we make no compromises with our dominion over ourselves, ever! It is a perfect rule that has saved me from countless temptations to give away my power. Absolute clarity about this and so much more. It has been an inspiration in my life and led me in many new spiritual directions. And now, I strive to live my life with the courage and love I fully recognized in Amorah, despite my imperfections.

Amorah in Mt. Shasta (2009)

More information about Amorah Quan Yin and the Dolphin Star Temple International can be found at:

http://www.amorahquanyin.com.

Printed in Great Britain
by Amazon